Python Excel Macros Scripts

Revolutionize Your Excel with Python-Powered Macros

Bryan Singer

3

Disclaimer

The information provided in this Book, "Python Excel Macros Scripts: Revolutionize Your Excel with Python-Powered Macros," is for educational and informational purposes only.

The content is intended to provide helpful and insightful guidance on utilizing Python to enhance Excel functionalities through macros.

This Book is designed to educate readers about Python and Excel macros. The techniques and examples provided are meant to illustrate concepts and should not be applied without careful consideration and testing in your specific environment.

While every effort has been made to ensure the accuracy and completeness of the information contained in this Book, the author makes no representations or warranties regarding its accuracy, completeness, or suitability for any particular purpose.

Discover Other Books in the Series

"Python for Excel Automation: Advanced techniques, complex Excel tasks"

"Python for Excel Data Analysis: Advanced Techniques, Automate Tasks"

"Python Excel for SQL: Efficiently Importing Excel Data with Panda"

"Python Excel External Data Sources: Integrate and Analyze Data from Any Source Seamlessly"

"Python Excel Dataframes: Advanced CSV Reading and Writing"

"Python Excel Cloud Online Tools: Learn How Python Can Transform Your Excel Experience in the Cloud"

"Python Excel Custom Report Generation: Creating Stunning Custom Reports with Ease"

Introduction

Welcome to "**Python Excel Macros Scripts: Revolutionize Your Excel with Python-Powered Macros**," the ultimate guide for anyone looking to supercharge their Excel capabilities using the power of Python. Whether you're a seasoned Python programmer, a web developer, a system administrator, a database manager, or a student eager to learn, this Book is designed to elevate your skills and transform the way you work with Excel.

In today's fast-paced digital world, efficiency and automation are key to staying ahead. Excel, a cornerstone tool in data management and analysis, offers tremendous potential, but many users barely scratch the surface of its capabilities. By harnessing the power of Python, you can unlock new dimensions of functionality, streamline your workflows, and achieve tasks that were once thought impossible.

This eBook delves into the fascinating intersection of Python and Excel, showing you how to create powerful macros that can automate repetitive tasks, process large datasets with ease, and integrate seamlessly with other applications. From basic scripting to advanced techniques, each chapter is packed with practical examples and step-by-step instructions that will help you master the art of Python-powered Excel macros.
You'll learn how to:

By the end of this Book, you'll not only have a solid understanding of how to write and implement Python macros in Excel, but you'll also be equipped with the skills to innovate and optimize your daily tasks like never before. Each chapter is designed to be engaging and accessible, ensuring that you can follow along and apply the concepts regardless of your starting level.

Get ready to revolutionize your Excel experience. Dive into the chapters that follow and discover how Python can transform your approach to data management, analysis, and automation. Your journey to becoming a Python Excel macro master starts here!

Chapter 1: Getting Started with Python and Excel

Excel, on the other hand, is the quintessential spreadsheet application that has been used in businesses, academia, and personal projects for decades. Combining the power of Python with the familiar interface of Excel unlocks a world of possibilities, allowing users to analyze data in ways previously unimaginable. In this chapter, we will explore the essentials of getting started with Python and Excel, covering installation, libraries, and basic operations.

1.1 Installing Python

To begin your journey into the realm of Python and Excel, you'll need to have Python installed on your system. Follow these steps for installation:

Download Python:

Visit the official Python website at [python.org](https://www.python.org/downloads/) and download the latest version suitable for your operating system (Windows, macOS, or Linux).

Install Python:

Run the installer and follow the instructions. Make sure to check the option "Add Python to PATH" before proceeding with the installation. This will allow you to run Python from the command line.

Verify Installation:

Open your terminal (Command Prompt on Windows, Terminal on macOS/Linux) and type:

```bash
python --version
```

This command should return the installed Python version, confirming that the installation was successful.

Install a Code Editor:

While you can write Python code in any text editor, using an Integrated Development Environment (IDE) can significantly improve your productivity. Popular options include:

VS Code: A powerful, lightweight code editor with numerous extensions for Python.

PyCharm: A feature-rich IDE specifically designed for Python development.

Jupyter Notebook: Excellent for interactive coding, particularly in data science and exploratory data analysis.

1.2 Setting Up Excel

If you're already familiar with Microsoft Excel, you're in great shape. If not, here's a brief overview:

Install Microsoft Excel:

Ensure you have Microsoft Excel installed. It's part of the Microsoft Office suite, which you may need to purchase or subscribe to via Office 365.

Explore Basic Functions:

Familiarize yourself with basic functions such as SUM, AVERAGE, VLOOKUP, and pivot tables, as they will complement the tasks you perform using Python.

1.3 Python Libraries for Excel

Python has several powerful libraries designed specifically for working with Excel files. Here are the most notable:

Pandas:

Pandas is an open-source data manipulation and analysis library. It provides data structures, such as DataFrames and Series, which make it easy to manipulate and analyze structured data.

```bash
pip install pandas
```

OpenPyXL:

OpenPyXL is a library that allows you to read and write Excel 2010 xlsx/xlsm/xltx/xltm files. It's particularly useful for creating and modifying Excel files programmatically.

```bash
pip install openpyxl
```

xlrd and xlwt:

These libraries are used for reading and writing older Excel files (xls format). However, since they don't support the newer xlsx format, OpenPyXL is usually preferred.

```bash
pip install xlrd xlwt
```

```
```

Matplotlib and Seaborn:

Though not directly related to Excel, these libraries are great for data visualization and often used in tandem with pandas for preparing data for presentation in Excel.

```bash
pip install matplotlib seaborn
```

1.4 Reading and Writing Excel Files

Let's illustrate how to read from and write to Excel files using pandas and OpenPyXL. ### Reading an Excel File

Assuming you have an Excel file named `sales_data.xlsx` with some sales records, use pandas to read the file:

```python
import pandas as pd
# Reading the Excel file
df = pd.read_excel('sales_data.xlsx')


# Display the first few rows print(df.head())
```

Writing to an Excel File

Building on the same dataset, suppose you want to filter the DataFrame and save it back to a new Excel file:

```python
```

```
# Filtering data for a specific condition filtered_data =
df[df['Sales'] > 1000]
```

```
# Writing to a new Excel file
filtered_data.to_excel('filtered_sales_data.xlsx',
index=False)
```

1.5 Basic Data Manipulation with Pandas

Pandas offers a variety of functionalities for data manipulation. Some of the basic operations include:

Sorting:

```python
sorted_data = df.sort_values(by='Sales', ascending=False)
```

Grouping:

```python
group_data = df.groupby('Region')['Sales'].sum()
```

Adding New Columns:

```python
df['Profit'] = df['Sales'] - df['Cost']
```

Data Visualization:

While not covered in Excel, data visualization is important to see trends:

```python
```

```
import matplotlib.pyplot as plt

df['Sales'].plot(kind='bar')  plt.title('Sales by Region')
plt.show()
```
` ` `

As we continue our journey in the following chapters, we'll explore more complex data manipulation techniques and discover how to make the most of this powerful combination.

Installing Python and Required Libraries for Excel

Python has become one of the most popular programming languages due to its versatility, ease of use, and robust libraries. One of its powerful applications is in conjunction with Microsoft Excel, allowing users to automate tasks, perform complex data analysis, and create dynamic reports. This chapter will guide you through the installation of Python and the essential libraries you will need to work seamlessly with Excel.

1. Understanding the Requirements

Before we dive into the installation process, let's outline the basic requirements:

Operating System: Python can be installed on various operating systems (Windows, macOS, Linux). Ensure you have the appropriate version for your system.

Excel: Depending on your needs, you may require a version of Microsoft Excel that supports Office Scripts or has Python integration (Excel 365 is recommended).

Internet Connection: An internet connection is essential for downloading Python, libraries, and packages.

2. Installing Python

Step 1: Downloading Python

Visit the official Python website: [python.org](https://www.python.org).

Click on the "Downloads" section. The website usually detects your operating system and suggests the best version for you (e.g., Python 3.x).

Click on the download link to get the installer. ### Step 2: Running the Installer

Locate the downloaded installer file (it is typically in your 'Downloads' folder).

Run the installer:

On Windows: Double-click the installer.

On macOS: Open the `.pkg` file.

Important: Check the box that says "Add Python to PATH" before clicking "Install Now." This step allows you to run Python from any command prompt or terminal window.

Step 3: Completing the Installation

Wait for the installation to complete. Once finished, you should see a confirmation screen.

You can verify the installation by opening a command prompt (cmd on Windows or Terminal on macOS) and typing:

```bash
```

```
python --version
```

You should see the installed version of Python displayed.
3. Setting Up a Python Environment While you can directly install libraries globally, it is a good practice to use a virtual environment. This isolates project dependencies and prevents version conflicts.

Step 1: Installing `venv`
`venv` is a lightweight tool for creating virtual environments that comes included with Python 3.3 and later. To create a virtual environment:

Open your command prompt or terminal.

Run the following command to create a new directory for your project:

```bash
mkdir my_excel_project cd my_excel_project
```

Create a virtual environment:

```bash
python -m venv env
```

Step 2: Activating the Virtual Environment To start using your virtual environment:
- **On Windows**:

```bash
```

```
.\env\Scripts\activate
```

- **On macOS/Linux**:
```bash
source env/bin/activate
```

Once activated, your command prompt will show the name of the environment (e.g., `(env)`), indicating that any packages you install will be isolated from the global Python installation.

4. Installing Required Libraries

Python's power comes from its libraries. For working with Excel, two libraries are particularly important:

`pandas` and `openpyxl`. ### Step 1: Installing Pandas

1. With your virtual environment activated, install `pandas` by running the following command:

```bash
pip install pandas
```

`pandas` is a library that provides data manipulation and analysis tools. ### Step 2: Installing openpyxl

1. Next, install `openpyxl`, which allows you to read from and write to Excel files (.xlsx):

```bash
pip install openpyxl
```

Step 3: Verifying Installation

To verify that the libraries have been installed correctly, open a Python session by typing `python` in your command line and then run the following commands:

```python
import pandas as pd import openpyxl

print("Pandas version:", pd.__version__) print("openpyxl version:", openpyxl.__version__)
```

If there are no errors and the versions print out, you have successfully installed the required libraries!

With `pandas` and `openpyxl`, you can now start manipulating and analyzing Excel data with the power of Python. In the following chapters, we will explore how to use these libraries to automate tasks, generate reports, and perform complex data analysis, thereby unleashing your productivity and capability with Excel. Keep your environment active as we embark on this exciting journey into the world of Python and Excel!

Setting Up Your Excel Environment in python

As data analysis continues to gain traction across industries, Python has emerged as a powerful tool for handling data, with libraries that simplify the process of interacting with Excel files. In this chapter, we'll guide you through setting up your Excel environment in Python, equipping you with the essential tools and knowledge to streamline your data manipulation and analysis tasks.

1. Introduction to Python for Excel

Python provides several libraries designed for reading, writing, and manipulating Excel files. The two most popular libraries are **Pandas** and **OpenPyXL**. Pandas is ideal for data analysis, while OpenPyXL focuses on complex tasks involving Excel file formats such as `.xlsx`. Understanding how to set up your environment with these libraries will enable you to manage your Excel files efficiently.

2. Installing Python

Before diving into the libraries, ensure you have Python installed on your computer. Follow these steps:

Download Python:

Visit the official Python website [python.org](https://www.python.org/downloads/).

Download the latest version compatible with your operating system.

Installation:

During the installation, ensure you check the box labeled **"Add Python to PATH."**

Proceed through the installation wizard to complete the setup.

Verify the Installation:

Open your command prompt or terminal and type:

```bash
python --version
```

This command should return the version of Python you installed. ### 3. Setting Up a Virtual Environment

Using a virtual environment helps you manage dependencies for different projects separately, preventing conflicts between packages. Here's how to set it up:

Create a virtual environment:

Navigate to the project directory where you want to set up your Python environment. Use the following command:

```bash
python -m venv excel-env
```

Activate the virtual environment:

- On Windows:

```bash
excel-env\Scripts\activate
```

- On macOS/Linux:

```bash
source excel-env/bin/activate
```

Verify Activation:

Once activated, your command prompt should show the name of the environment in parentheses. ### 4. Installing Required Libraries

With the virtual environment active, you can install the libraries needed for Excel manipulation.

Pandas:

Pandas offers data structures and data analysis tools. Install it using pip:

```bash
pip install pandas
```

OpenPyXL:

This library helps you read and write Excel 2010 xlsx/xlsm/xltx/xltm files. Install it by running:

```bash
pip install openpyxl
```

Additional Libraries:

Depending on your use case, you may also want to install:
- **NumPy** for numerical operations:

```bash
```

```bash
pip install numpy
```

- **Matplotlib** or **Seaborn** for plotting:
```bash
pip install matplotlib seaborn
```

5. Testing Your Setup

To ensure everything is working correctly, create a simple Python script that imports the libraries and performs a basic operation.

Create a new Python file:

Open any code editor and create a file named `test_excel.py`.

Write the following code:

```python
import pandas as pd


# Creating a simple DataFrame data = {
'Name': ['Alice', 'Bob', 'Charlie'], 'Age': [25, 30, 35]
}
df = pd.DataFrame(data)


# Saving the DataFrame to an Excel file
df.to_excel('test.xlsx', index=False)
```

```
print("Excel file created successfully!")
```

Run the script: In your terminal, run:

```bash
python test_excel.py
```

If you see the message "Excel file created successfully!" and a file named `test.xlsx` appears in your directory, congratulations! Your Excel environment is set up correctly.

6. Common Challenges and Troubleshooting

Module Not Found Error:

If you encounter an error stating that the module is not found, ensure that you installed the library in the active virtual environment.

Permission Errors:

Running scripts that create or write files in certain directories may require elevated permissions. Try running your terminal as an administrator.

Compatibility Issues:

If you are using older versions of Excel or Python, certain features may not work as expected. Always refer to the official documentation for compatibility notes.

Having a well-structured Excel environment in Python sets the foundation for effective data analysis. By installing the necessary libraries and understanding how to manipulate Excel files using Python, you will enhance your productivity and simplify your workflow.

Chapter 2: Understanding Excel VBA Macros

Excel is widely recognized for its robust capabilities in data analysis, organization, and visualization. However, the true powerhouse of Excel lies in its ability to automate repetitive tasks through Excel VBA (Visual Basic for Applications) macros. In this chapter, we will explore the fundamentals of VBA macros, their architecture, how to write them, and how to implement them in your daily Excel tasks.

What are VBA Macros?

VBA macros are a series of instructions that automate tasks within Excel. They can perform complex calculations, manipulate data, and generate reports with just a button click. The core purpose of macros is to save time and increase efficiency, enabling users to focus on higher-level analytical tasks rather than mundane operations.

Why Use Macros?

Efficiency: Macros can perform tasks much faster than a human can. A routine task that takes minutes can be reduced to seconds.

Repetitive Tasks: For tasks that need to be performed multiple times, such as formatting reports or updating data, macros eliminate the need to repeat the same steps, thus reducing human error.

Complex Operations: Some tasks can involve complex calculations or data manipulation. Macros can encapsulate these actions into a single command.

Customized Solutions: VBA allows you to tailor macros to fit your specific needs, making them versatile tools in any business intelligence toolkit.

The Anatomy of a VBA Macro

Understanding how VBA macros are structured is essential for writing and debugging them. Let's break down a simple macro example:

```vba
Sub HelloWorld() MsgBox "Hello, World!"
End Sub
```

Sub: This keyword indicates the beginning of a macro. It defines a subroutine (a block of code that performs a specific task).

HelloWorld: This is the name of the macro. It should be descriptive for clarity.

MsgBox: This function triggers a message box to display a dialog to the user. In this case, it shows the message "Hello, World!".

End Sub: This keyword signifies the end of the macro, encapsulating the actions within the subroutine. ## Creating Your First Macro

In Excel, creating a macro can be accomplished through the following steps:

Open the Developer Tab: If the Developer tab is not visible, enable it through Excel Options. Go to File > Options > Customize Ribbon and check the Developer option.

Record a Macro: Click on "Record Macro" in the Developer tab. You will be prompted to give your macro a name, assign a shortcut key (optional), and choose where to store it.

Perform Actions: As you record, perform the tasks you wish to automate. Excel captures each action.

Stop Recording: Once you've completed your actions, click on "Stop Recording." Your macro is now created.

View the Code: To see the generated VBA code, click on "Visual Basic" in the Developer tab. You'll find your macro under "Modules."

Editing a Macro

After creating a macro, you may want to customize it. Here's how to edit:

Open the Visual Basic for Applications Editor: This can be done by clicking "Visual Basic" on the Developer tab.

Locate Your Module: In the editor, find the module that contains your macro.

Edit the Code: Make changes directly in the code window. Ensure you understand the syntax to avoid errors.

Test the Macro: It is essential to test your macro after making changes. You can run it directly from the VBA editor or return to Excel.

Debugging Macros

While writing VBA code, encountering errors is commonplace. The following techniques can help debug your macros:

Error Messages: Pay attention to error messages that Excel may display. They often provide hints about where the issue lies.

Breakpoint: You can set breakpoints in your code by clicking in the margin next to a line. This will pause the execution, allowing you to step through your code.

Step Through Code: Use F8 to step through your macro line by line. This helps identify where the code might be misbehaving.

Immediate Window: In the VBA editor, you can use the Immediate Window (View > Immediate Window) to test code snippets and check variable values in real-time.

Best Practices for Writing VBA Macros

Comment Your Code: Use comments to explain sections of your macro. This is particularly helpful for future reference or when sharing your work with others.

Use Descriptive Names: Name your macros and variables descriptively to make the code self- explanatory.

Limit Scope: Keep macros focused on a single task or function. This makes testing and debugging simpler.

Avoid Hardcoding Values: If possible, use cell references or named ranges instead of hardcoding values. This makes your macro flexible and easier to maintain.

Back Up Your Work: Always save a backup of your workbook before running new macros to avoid data loss.

Excel VBA macros are powerful tools that can significantly enhance productivity and streamline workflows. In this chapter, we covered the basics of understanding and creating VBA macros, the structure of a macro, how to edit and debug them, and best practices for writing effective code. As you become more comfortable with Excel VBA, you can leverage macros to create more complex automations tailored to your unique needs.

Basics of VBA Macros

Visual Basic for Applications (VBA) is a powerful programming language integrated into Microsoft Office applications, such as Excel, Word, and Access. It allows users to automate tasks, manipulate data, and enhance user productivity through the creation of macros. This chapter will introduce the basic concepts of VBA macros, their structure, and how you can leverage them to simplify your work processes.

What is a Macro?

A macro is a series of commands and functions that you can store and run whenever you need to perform a specific task. In Excel, for example, you might create a macro to automate repetitive tasks like formatting data, generating reports, or performing complex calculations. Macros help minimize errors and save valuable time by allowing users to execute complex sequences of tasks with a single command.

Why Use VBA Macros?

Automation: VBA macros can automate repetitive tasks, reducing the time and effort spent on manual entries.

Customization: Users can create custom functions and procedures that are tailored to their specific needs.

Improved Accuracy: Automating tasks can help eliminate human errors associated with manual processes.

Enhanced Functionality: With VBA, you can extend the capabilities of Excel and other Office applications beyond their basic functionalities.

Getting Started with VBA

To start using VBA macros, you must have access to the Developer tab in Excel or other Office applications. If you don't see the Developer tab, you can enable it by going to:

File -> **Options**.

Select **Customize Ribbon**.

Check the **Developer** checkbox on the right panel and click **OK**. ### The VBA Editor

To create a macro, you'll need to access the Visual Basic for Applications (VBA) editor:

Click on the **Developer** tab.

Click on the **Visual Basic** button. This opens the VBA editor where you will write your code. ### Creating Your First Macro

Creating a simple macro begins with recording actions or writing code manually. Here's how to record a macro:

On the Developer tab, click **Record Macro**.

Provide a name for your macro, ensuring it begins with a letter and contains no spaces (e.g., `FormatReport`).

Choose a shortcut key if desired, then select where to store the macro (This Workbook, New Workbook, or Personal Macro Workbook).

Perform the actions you want to automate.

Click **Stop Recording** when done.

Alternatively, you can write the macro directly in the VBA editor:

In the VBA editor, locate the project tree on the left.

Right-click on the workbook where you want to add the macro and select **Insert** -> **Module**.

In the new module window, you can write your VBA code. For example:

```vba
Sub FormatReport()

With ThisWorkbook.Sheets("Sheet1")

.Range("A1:A10").Font.Bold = True

.Range("A1:A10").Interior.Color = RGB(255, 255, 0) ' Yellow background End With
```

End Sub
```

Save your work by clicking the disk icon or using **Ctrl + S**. ## Understanding the VBA Syntax

VBA has a straightforward syntax resembling other programming languages but unique in certain aspects. Here are some key components:

### Variables

Variables are used to store data values. You can declare a variable using the `Dim` statement:

```vba

Dim count As Integer count = 10
```

Data Types

Common data types include:

Integer: Whole numbers.

Double: Floating-point numbers.

String: Text.

Boolean: True/False values. ### Control Structures

Control structures determine the flow of execution. Common structures include:

If...Then...Else:

```vba

If count > 5 Then

MsgBox "Count is greater than 5" Else

32
```
```

MsgBox "Count is 5 or less" End If

```

```

For Loop:

```vba
For i = 1 To 10

Debug.Print i ' Outputs numbers 1 through 10 to the Immediate window Next i
```

Debugging Your Macros

Debugging is an essential part of programming. The VBA editor has debugging tools, including:

Breakpoints: Allows you to pause execution at a specific line of code.

Step Into: Execute your code one line at a time.

Immediate Window: Used to test code snippets and check variable values during execution. To set a breakpoint, click in the margin next to the line of code where you want execution to pause.

Whether you're looking to simplify data entry, automate reporting, or develop complex data analysis tools, learning to create and manipulate VBA macros will undoubtedly elevate your efficiency. As you gain confidence, you can explore more advanced features of VBA, unlocking even greater potential in your everyday tasks.

Common VBA Practices and Pitfalls

Visual Basic for Applications (VBA) remains one of the most powerful tools for automating tasks within Microsoft Office applications such as Excel, Word, and Access. While the potential to streamline processes is vast, there are common practices that can enhance code quality, performance, and usability, as well as several pitfalls that can lead to frustrating results. This chapter explores both the best practices to adopt and the common pitfalls to avoid when working with VBA.

Common VBA Practices

1. Use Meaningful Naming Conventions

Clear and meaningful variable and procedure names are critical in any programming language, and VBA is no exception. Using descriptive names for your modules, functions, variables, and constants can make your code easier to understand and maintain. For instance, instead of naming a variable `x`, consider something more descriptive like `totalSales`, which indicates what the variable is used for.

Example:

```vba
Dim totalSales As Double
```

2. Comment Your Code

Comments help document your code, making it easier for others (or yourself) to understand its functionality in the future. Use comments to describe what a procedure does, what a complex piece of code is intended for, and any assumptions that you make.

Example:

```vba
' This procedure calculates the total sales for the month
Sub CalculateTotalSales()

' Variable to hold the total sales Dim totalSales As Double

' Code for calculation goes here... End Sub
```

3. Error Handling

Implementing robust error handling in your VBA code can help manage unexpected situations gracefully. Use the `On Error` statements to catch and manage errors, ensuring your program can continue or shut down gracefully.

Example:

```vba
Sub SafeDivide()

On Error GoTo ErrorHandler Dim result As Double

result = 10 / 0 ' This will raise a divide by zero error Exit Sub
```

ErrorHandler:

MsgBox "An error occurred: " & Err.Description End Sub
```

### 4. Avoid Hardcoding Values

Hardcoding values directly into your code can lead to maintenance issues down the line. Instead, use constants or retrieve values from cells or user inputs. This approach not only makes your code cleaner but also allows easier adjustments in future iterations without delving into the code.

#### Example:

```vba
Const TAX_RATE As Double = 0.075
```

5. Keep Code Modular

Breaking your code into small, manageable procedures—or modules—can improve readability and reusability. This modular approach makes it easier to test pieces of code independently and makes debugging simpler.

Example:

```vba
Sub Main()
Call CalculateTotalSales Call GenerateReport
End Sub
Sub CalculateTotalSales() ' Implementation here...
End Sub
```

36
```

```
Sub GenerateReport()
' Implementation here... End Sub
```

6. Use Option Explicit

At the top of your modules, use `Option Explicit`. This forces you to declare all your variables explicitly, which can help prevent errors stemming from typos and ensure that your code is more readable.

Example:

```vba
Option Explicit

Sub ExampleSub()

Dim count As Integer

' The rest of your code... End Sub
```

Common VBA Pitfalls

1. Ignoring Data Types

VBA is not as strict with data types compared to other languages, which can lead to unexpected behavior or errors. Always declare the correct data type for your variables to ensure correct operations and optimize performance.

2. Not Utilizing Debugging Tools

Many developers overlook the debugging tools provided in the VBA editor. Make use of features like breakpoints, the immediate window, and step-through execution to trace through your code and identify mistakes.

3. Failing to Optimize Performance

It's easy to forget about performance when writing VBA, especially in larger projects or with complex calculations. Using inefficient loops or not taking advantage of array operations can lead to slow-running applications. Always consider optimal solutions, such as using `For Each` for collections or working with arrays instead of cell-by-cell operations when possible.

Poor Example:

```vba
For i = 1 To 100

Cells(i, 1).Value = i * 2 Next i
```

Optimized Example:

```vba
Dim data(1 To 100) As Integer For i = 1 To 100
```

data(i) = i * 2 Next i

Application.WorksheetFunction.Transpose(data)

```
```

4. Overusing Select and Activate

Many novice VBA programmers rely heavily on the `Select` and `Activate` methods, believing them necessary to manipulate objects. This can lead to slower performance and makes code unnecessarily complicated. Instead, directly reference the objects you need.

Poor Example:

```vba
Sheets("Sheet1").Select    Range("A1").Select
ActiveCell.Value = "Hello"
```

Improved Example:

```vba
Sheets("Sheet1").Range("A1").Value = "Hello"
```

5. Not Saving Regularly

VBA projects can occasionally crash, and if you have not saved your work regularly, you risk losing significant amounts of code. It's advisable to use version control or at least save your project frequently.

6. Overlooking the User's Experience

When designing macros or applications, don't los sight of the end-user experience. Consider how users will interact with your application, provide clear error messages, guide them through the process, and create intuitive UIs where applicable.

By adhering to common practices and avoiding pitfalls, you can make your VBA programming more effective and enjoyable. Striving for clean, readable, and error-resistant code will not only streamline your work but also help you become a stronger programmer overall. As you gain more experience with VBA, you'll develop a deeper understanding of its nuances, but remember: the best coding practices will serve you well throughout your programming journey.

Chapter 3: Translating VBA Macros to Python

Python's simplicity, versatility, and extensive libraries provide a more comprehensive approach to data manipulation, making it an ideal choice for those looking to enhance their capabilities. This chapter will guide you through the process of translating VBA macros to Python, showcasing practical examples that highlight both languages' similarities and differences.

3.1 Understanding VBA Macros

Before we delve into the comparison between VBA and Python, it's essential to understand the function of VBA macros. VBA is primarily used for automating repetitive tasks in Excel, allowing users to create custom functions, enhance user interfaces, and build interactive spreadsheets. A typical VBA macro consists of a series of commands written in a procedural format, where each command instructs Excel to perform specific actions, such as manipulating data or controlling workbook behavior.

For instance, consider a simple VBA macro that calculates the sum of a range of cells:

```vba
Sub SumRange()

Dim total As Double

total = Application.WorksheetFunction.Sum(Range("A1:A10"))
MsgBox "The total is: " & total

End Sub
```

```
```

This macro defines a `Sub` procedure named `SumRange`, calculates the sum of the values in cells A1 through A10, and displays the result in a message box.

3.2 Introduction to Python

Python, on the other hand, is a high-level programming language known for its readability and ease of use. With a rich set of libraries (like `pandas`, `openpyxl`, and `numpy`), Python offers robust data manipulation capabilities that surpass those of VBA. For Excel-specific tasks, the `openpyxl` and `pandas` libraries are particularly useful, allowing you to read, write, and process Excel files seamlessly.

3.3 Translating Basic VBA Concepts to Python

To translate the VBA macro into Python, we'll break down the essential components and examine how to implement them using Python syntax.

3.3.1 Variable Declaration

VBA declares variables using the `Dim` statement while Python handles variable declarations dynamically:

VBA:

```vba
Dim total As Double
```

Python:

```python
```

```
total = 0.0
```

3.3.2 Working with Ranges

In VBA, you refer to cell ranges directly using the `Range` object. In Python with `openpyxl`, you access ranges through worksheet objects:

VBA:

```vba
total = Application.WorksheetFunction.Sum(Range("A1:A10"))
```

Python:

```python
import openpyxl

workbook = openpyxl.load_workbook('example.xlsx')
sheet = workbook.active

total = sum(cell.value for cell in sheet['A1:A10'])
```

3.3.3 Displaying Messages

In VBA, the `MsgBox` function is commonly used to display messages to users. In Python, you can utilize the `print()` function or libraries like `tkinter` for more complex user interfaces.

VBA:

```vba
MsgBox "The total is: " & total
```

```
` ` `
```

Python:

```python
print(f"The total is: {total}")
```

3.4 Complete Python Example

Putting it all together, here's how the entire VBA macro `SumRange` can be translated into Python:

```python
import openpyxl

def sum_range(filename):
    # Load the workbook and select the active worksheet
    workbook = openpyxl.load_workbook(filename) sheet = workbook.active
    # Calculate the sum of the specified range
    total = sum(cell.value for cell in sheet['A1:A10'])


    # Display the result print(f"The total is: {total}")


    # Usage sum_range('example.xlsx')
```

3.5 Leveraging Python Libraries

One of the hallmark features of Python is its rich ecosystem of libraries and frameworks. By leveraging libraries like `pandas`, you can streamline data processing even further. Here's how the same task could be accomplished using `pandas`:

```python
import pandas as pd

def sum_range_with_pandas(filename):
# Load the Excel file into a DataFrame df = pd.read_excel(filename)

# Calculate the total of the specified range
total = df['A'].sum()  # Assuming the data is in column 'A'

# Display the result print(f"The total is: {total}")
# Usage sum_range_with_pandas('example.xlsx')
```

3.6 Conclusion

Translating VBA macros to Python is an invaluable skill for modern analysts and developers. While the two languages offer different syntaxes and structures, their core functionalities often align closely, enabling seamless migrations of automation tasks.

As you continue to explore the capabilities of Python, you'll discover even more ways to enhance your data processing tasks, utilizing the extensive libraries and community support that Python provides. This chapter serves as a stepping stone to adopting Python for your automation and data analysis needs, paving the way for more complex projects and sophisticated data manipulation.

3.7 Further Practices

To solidify your understanding of translating VBA to Python, consider implementing the following exercises:

Conditional Logic: Translate a VBA macro that includes `If...Then` statements into Python using `if` statements.

Loops: Practice converting `For` loops and `While` loops from VBA to Python.

User Input: Create Python scripts that mimic user prompts in Excel via Input Boxes in VBA.

These exercises will help you gain confidence in transitioning from VBA to Python, unlocking a powerful toolkit for your programming needs.

Key Differences Between VBA and Python

While both serve the fundamental purpose of automating tasks, manipulating data, and enhancing productivity, they differ significantly in their design philosophy, syntax, ecosystem, and areas of application. This chapter explores the key differences between VBA and Python, providing insights that can help users choose the right tool for their specific needs.

1. Language Design and Syntax

VBA:

VBA, a derivative of Visual Basic, was designed primarily for automating tasks within Microsoft Office applications such as Excel, Word, and Access. Its syntax is more verbose, which can make it somewhat cumbersome for complex programming tasks. For example, declaring a variable in VBA involves specifying its type explicitly.

```vba
Dim total as Integer total = 0
```

VBA's design encourages a more structured and event-driven approach, closely tied to the user interface elements of Office applications. The focus is often on interaction with application objects, making it intuitive for users familiar with Microsoft products.

Python:

In contrast, Python is a general-purpose programming language known for its elegant syntax and readability. Its design philosophy emphasizes code clarity and simplicity, allowing programmers to express concepts in fewer lines of code. Variable declaration in Python is implicit, which adds to its ease of use.

```python
total = 0
```

Python's syntax is consistent and less rigid, enabling rapid development and experimentation. This makes it a favorite among beginners as well as experienced developers who value productivity and maintainability.

2. Platform Dependency

VBA:

VBA is inherently tied to the Windows operating system and specifically to Microsoft Office applications. This dependency restricts its use to environments where these applications are installed. While it can be a powerful tool for automating tasks within Office, it lacks the versatility needed for cross-platform development.

Python:

Python is a cross-platform language that can run on various operating systems, including Windows, macOS, and Linux. This flexibility allows developers to build applications that are independent of specific software environments, making Python suitable for web development, data science, machine learning, and more.

Python's wide-ranging capabilities enable it to integrate with various APIs and libraries, enhancing its usability across diverse fields.

3. Libraries and Ecosystem

VBA:

VBA has a limited ecosystem, primarily focused around Microsoft Office applications. While it does have libraries for automating tasks within these applications, the options for external libraries are restricted. Users often find themselves limited when trying to tackle complex tasks that require advanced functionalities outside of the Office suite.

Python:

Python boasts a rich and extensive ecosystem of libraries and frameworks that cater to almost every need. From data analysis with Pandas and NumPy to web development with Flask and Django, and machine learning with TensorFlow and scikit-learn, Python's libraries enable robust functionality and versatility. This massive repository of third-party libraries allows users to expand their projects well beyond the capabilities of VBA.

4. Community and Support

VBA:

Although VBA has been around for many years and has a dedicated community, the number of active contributors has diminished compared to modern programming languages. The community tends to focus on specific Microsoft products, and while many resources exist, they are often less diverse and less comprehensive than those available for languages like Python.

Python:

Python has one of the largest and most vibrant programming communities. The language's popularity has fostered a wealth of resources, tutorials, forums, and open-source projects. The support from both the community and official documentation makes troubleshooting and learning much more accessible, creating a welcoming environment for new learners and seasoned developers alike.

5. Application Domains

VBA:

VBA is primarily used for automating tasks within Microsoft Office applications. It excels in scenarios where users need quick automation solutions for data analysis, reporting, and repetitive tasks. It's particularly popular among business analysts and financial professionals who work in finance and accounting and rely heavily on Excel for data manipulation.

Python:

Python's versatility allows it to thrive in a myriad of domains beyond office automation. It's widely used in web development, scientific computing, data analysis, artificial intelligence, and more. Python's flexibility means it can be employed in various environments, from small scripts to large-scale applications, making it suitable for both individuals and enterprises.

6. Learning Curve

VBA:

For users already familiar with Microsoft Office applications, learning VBA can be relatively easy since it builds on the existing knowledge of these tools. However, the lack of modern programming paradigms can hinder learning for those looking to advance beyond basic automation.

Python:

Python is widely regarded as one of the most beginner-friendly programming languages, thanks to its clear syntax and abundant resources. New developers can quickly grasp fundamental programming concepts and rapidly move on to more complex topics, fostering greater long-term growth.

For those working extensively within Microsoft Office who need to automate repetitive tasks, VBA can be an effective solution. However, for developers seeking versatility, a broader application scope, and a rich ecosystem, Python is typically the better choice. By understanding these key differences, users can make informed decisions when selecting the right tool for their needs, maximizing productivity and efficiency in their workflows.

Step-by-Step Conversion VBA Macros to Python

Visual Basic for Applications (VBA) has long been a go-to scripting language for automating tasks in Microsoft Excel and other Office applications. However, as the programming landscape evolves, many developers and data analysts are transitioning to Python, a language known for its versatility, readability, and extensive libraries. In this chapter, we will provide a detailed guide on how to convert VBA macros to Python, making the transition smoother for those looking to harness the power of Python in their data processing and automation tasks.

Understanding the Basics

Before diving into the conversion process, it's important to understand both VBA and Python fundamentals. ### VBA Macros: A Quick Overview

VBA is an event-driven programming language that allows users to automate repetitive tasks in Excel and other MS Office applications. It uses a straightforward syntax that is closely tied to the Excel application. A typical VBA macro might look like this:

```vba
Sub ExampleMacro() Dim ws As Worksheet

Set ws = ThisWorkbook.Sheets("Sheet1") ws.Range("A1").Value = "Hello, World!"

End Sub
```

In this example, a sheet is referenced, and a value is set in cell A1. ### Python: A Versatile Language

Python, on the other hand, is a high-level programming language that is designed for readability and simplicity. With libraries like `pandas`, `openpyxl`, and `xlrd`, Python provides powerful tools for data manipulation and Excel file handling. An equivalent action in Python might look as follows:

```python
import pandas as pd

df = pd.DataFrame()

df.at[0, 'A'] = 'Hello, World!'
```

In this conversion, we create a DataFrame and set the value at a specific position. ## Step-by-Step Conversion Process

In this section, we will break down the conversion process into manageable steps. ### Step 1: Analyze the VBA Code

Before converting, thoroughly analyze the VBA code you wish to convert. Identify key components such as:

Worksheet references

Ranges and selections

Formulas and calculations

Loops and conditionals

User input and output

Step 2: Set Up Your Python Environment

To work with Excel files in Python, you'll need to set up your environment:

Install Python from the official [Python website](https://www.python.org/).

Install necessary libraries using pip:

```bash
pip install pandas openpyxl
```

Create a new Python script (`script.py`) where you will write your Python code. ### Step 3: Map VBA Functions to Python

Identify the VBA functions and control structures (like loops, conditions) used in your macros and find their Python counterparts:

VBA	**Python**

`If ... Then ... Else`	`if ... else:`
`For Each ... Next`	`for item in iterable:`
`Dim variable`	`variable = value`
`Set object = New Object`	`object = Object()`	### Step 4: Rewrite the Code in Python

Now that you have a good understanding of the VBA code and its equivalents in Python, start rewriting the code. Here's how to convert the earlier example:

54

VBA Code:

```vba
Sub ExampleMacro() Dim ws As Worksheet
Set ws = ThisWorkbook.Sheets("Sheet1")
ws.Range("A1").Value = "Hello, World!"
End Sub
```

Equivalent Python Code:

```python
import pandas as pd
# Creating a DataFrame to mimic the Excel Sheet
df = pd.DataFrame(index=range(10), columns=['A'])


# Setting value in cell A1 df.at[0, 'A'] = 'Hello, World!'
# Writing to an Excel file df.to_excel('output.xlsx',
index=False)
```

Step 5: Test the Python Code

Once you have converted your macro, test it thoroughly. Make sure that the output matches what you would have seen in Excel after running the VBA macro. You may need to refine your code based on the results.

Step 6: Optimize the Python Code

Python's efficiency can often lead to optimization opportunities. Use list comprehensions, lambda functions, and vectorized operations with `pandas` to streamline your code further. Compare the processing time of your VBA macro with the Python version, focusing on performance improvements.

Transitioning from VBA macros to Python can significantly enhance your data processing capabilities. With the step-by-step conversion process outlined in this chapter, you should now have a solid foundation for converting VBA code into Python scripts.

By leveraging Python's extensive libraries, you can not only replicate the functionality of your VBA macros but also expand upon them, making your data analysis and automation tasks far more powerful. As you gain experience in Python, you will discover new ways to optimize your code and simplify your workflows, ensuring that you keep up with the evolving landscape of data automation and analysis.

Further Reading

Python Official Documentation: [python.org](https://docs.python.org/3/)

pandas Documentation: [pandas.pydata.org](https://pandas.pydata.org/pandas-docs/stable/)

openpyxl Documentation: [openpyxl.readthedocs.io](https://openpyxl.readthedocs.io/en/stable/).

Chapter 4: Essential Python Libraries for Excel Automation

Python, with its extensive ecosystem of libraries, offers excellent options for automating tasks in Excel. In this chapter, we will explore some of the essential Python libraries that facilitate Excel automation, enabling you to manipulate, analyze, and visualize spreadsheet data effectively.

4.1 Overview of Python Libraries for Excel

Python has several libraries tailored specifically for working with Excel files, each catering to different needs and offering various functionalities. Some of the most prominent libraries include:

Pandas

OpenPyXL

XlsxWriter

xlrd and **xlwt**

Pywin32 (win32com)

pyexcel

Let's delve deeper into each of these libraries to understand their features and use cases. ## 4.2 Pandas

Pandas is one of the most widely used Python libraries for data manipulation and analysis, and it can handle Excel files seamlessly.

Features:

DataFrame Manipulation: Pandas enables you to read Excel files into a DataFrame, perform operations like filtering, sorting, grouping, and aggregation with ease.

Read/Write Support: It supports reading from and writing to Excel files using formats like `.xls` and

`.xlsx`.

Integration with Other Libraries: Pandas integrates well with libraries like NumPy and Matplotlib, allowing for advanced data analysis and visualization.

Example Usage:

```python
import pandas as pd
# Read an Excel file
df = pd.read_excel('data.xlsx', sheet_name='Sheet1')
# Perform data manipulation df['New_Column'] = df['Old_Column'] * 2
# Write the modified DataFrame back to Excel df.to_excel('modified_data.xlsx', index=False)
```

4.3 OpenPyXL

OpenPyXL is a library specifically designed for reading and writing Excel 2010 files in the `.xlsx` format. It is particularly useful for creating complex spreadsheets and formatting cells.

Features:

Cell Formatting: You can easily format cells, change colors, fonts, and styles.

Charts: OpenPyXL allows you to create and customize charts within your Excel files.

Support for Formulas: You can programmatically set formulas and manipulate Excel features.

Example Usage:

```python
from openpyxl import Workbook

# Create a new workbook and select the active worksheet
wb = Workbook()

ws = wb.active

# Write data to cells ws['A1'] = "Hello"

ws['A2'] = "World"

# Save the workbook wb.save('sample.xlsx')
```

4.4 XlsxWriter

XlsxWriter is another library that allows you to write data to Excel 2010 files (`.xlsx`). Unlike OpenPyXL, XlsxWriter is focused on writing data and does not support reading or modifying existing files.

Features:

Formatting: Offers extensive formatting options for cells, including colors, borders, and number formats.

Advanced Charting: Exceptional capabilities for adding charts and other visual elements to spreadsheets.

Performance: Highly optimized for writing large datasets.

Example Usage:

```python
import xlsxwriter
# Create a new Excel file
workbook = xlsxwriter.Workbook('charts.xlsx') worksheet = workbook.add_worksheet()
# Write some data worksheet.write('A1', 'Data') worksheet.write('A2', 123)
worksheet.write('A3', 456)
# Add a simple chart
chart = workbook.add_chart({'type': 'column'})
chart.add_series({'name': 'Data', 'values': '=Sheet1!$A$2:$A$3'}) worksheet.insert_chart('C1', chart)


# Close the workbook workbook.close()


```

4.5 xlrd and xlwt

These two libraries have been traditionally used for reading (xlrd) and writing (xlwt) Excel files in the older

`.xls` format. However, with advancements in file formats and newer libraries, their use has declined. Nonetheless, they can still be valuable for legacy support.

Example Usage of xlrd:

```python
import xlrd
# Open an existing workbook
workbook = xlrd.open_workbook('data.xls')
sheet = workbook.sheet_by_index(0)
# Read data from the first column
for row in range(sheet.nrows):
    print(sheet.cell_value(row, 0))
```

Example Usage of xlwt:

```python
import xlwt
# Create a workbook and add a sheet
workbook = xlwt.Workbook()
sheet = workbook.add_sheet('Sheet 1')
# Write data
sheet.write(0, 0, 'Hello')
sheet.write(0, 1, 'World')
# Save the workbook
workbook.save('output.xls')
```

4.6 Pywin32 (win32com)

For Windows users, Pywin32 allows you to interact with Excel through its COM interface. This can be particularly useful for automating Excel on Windows systems.

Features:

Full Excel Control: You can manipulate Excel more thoroughly, controlling the application itself.

Macro Automation: Useful for automating tasks that

are usually handled through Excel's own macro functionalities.

Example Usage:

```python
import win32com.client
# Start an instance of Excel
excel = win32com.client.Dispatch('Excel.Application')

# Make Excel visible excel.Visible = True
# Add a new workbook
workbook = excel.Workbooks.Add()
# Write to a cell
workbook.Worksheets(1).Cells(1, 1).Value = "Hello, Excel!"
# Save and close workbook.SaveAs('automated_excel.xlsx')
workbook.Close()
excel.Quit()
```

4.7 pyexcel

Pyexcel is a library that supports reading, writing, and manipulating Excel files (among other formats) in a unified way. It focuses on providing a simple, high-level interface.

Features:

Unified API: Works with various formats like `.xls`,

`.xlsx`, and `.ods`.

Lightweight and Simple: Ideal for quick data handling without the overhead of complex features.

Example Usage:

```python
import pyexcel as pe
# Load an existing spreadsheet
book = pe.get_book(file_name='data.xlsx')
# Access a specific sheet sheet = book['Sheet1']
# Read data from the sheet data = sheet.to_array()
# Manipulate data and save it data[0][0] = "Updated Value" book.save_as('updated_data.xlsx')
```

In this chapter, we explored several essential Python libraries for automating tasks in Excel, each with its unique strengths and features. Whether you are performing data analysis with Pandas, creating complex spreadsheets with OpenPyXL or XlsxWriter, managing legacy files with xlrd and xlwt, or automating tasks with Pywin32, these libraries empower you to leverage the full potential of Excel.

Introduction to pandas, openpyxl, and xlwings

Python, with its rich ecosystem of libraries, has emerged as a powerful tool for data manipulation and analysis. In this chapter, we will explore three prominent libraries: **Pandas**, **Openpyxl**, and

Xlwings. Each of these tools plays a crucial role in handling data, especially in relation to Excel spreadsheets, which remain one of the most ubiquitous tools for data management.

1.1 Understanding Pandas

Pandas is an open-source data manipulation and analysis library built on top of the Python programming language. It provides two primary data structures: Series and DataFrame.

Series: A one-dimensional labeled array capable of holding any data type (integers, floats, strings, Python objects, etc.). It is similar to a column in a spreadsheet.

DataFrame: A two-dimensional labeled data structure that can store data of different types (similar to a table in a database or a spreadsheet). DataFrames allow for easy manipulation, filtering, and transformation of data.

Pandas shines in its ability to perform complex data transformations with just a few lines of code. It provides functions for data filtering, grouping, merging, and reshaping, making it ideal for exploratory data analysis.

Key Features of Pandas:

Fast and efficient for data manipulation and analysis.

Built-in support for handling missing data.

Powerful data aggregation functions.

Support for time series data.

Easy integration with other data visualization libraries such as Matplotlib and Seaborn. ## 1.2 Introduction to Openpyxl

Openpyxl is a Python library used to read and write Excel files (.xlsx format). Unlike Pandas, which is primarily used for data analysis, Openpyxl is designed specifically for manipulating Excel files at a more granular level.

With Openpyxl, you can perform tasks such as:

Creating new Excel files and sheets.

Modifying existing Excel files by changing cell values, styles, and formulas.

Reading data from Excel files into Python for further processing.

Writing data from Python back into Excel files.

Openpyxl is particularly useful when you need to create reports that require formatting and styling beyond what is possible with standard DataFrames. It allows you to control font styles, borders, cell colors, and more—turning data analysis outputs into professional-grade reports directly within Excel.

Key Features of Openpyxl:

Ability to read, write, and modify Excel files (.xlsx).

Support for advanced Excel features like charts and conditional formatting.

Compatibility with large datasets.

Option for creating pivot tables programmatically.

1.3 Getting to Know Xlwings

Xlwings is a powerful Python library that bridges the gap between Python and Excel, providing the ability to call Python code from Excel and vice versa. It acts as a bridge, allowing users to leverage Python's rich data manipulation capabilities within the familiar Excel interface.

Why Use Xlwings?

Interactivity: You can update Excel spreadsheets dynamically using Python scripts and see the results in real-time.

User-defined Functions: You can define Python functions and call them from within Excel as if they were regular Excel functions.

Data Exchange: Xlwings allows for easy reading and writing of data between Excel and Python, making it easier to perform complex calculations or analyses with Python's libraries (like Pandas).

In an environment where Excel is often the first tool for data analysis, Xlwings empowers users to combine the flexibility and power of Python with the usability of Excel, fundamentally transforming how analyses are conducted.

Key Features of Xlwings:

Seamless integration with Excel for real-time data manipulation.

Capability to create Excel add-ins using Python.

Ability to generate Excel reports automatically.

Support for working with large datasets efficiently.

In the chapters to follow, we will delve deeper into each library, providing practical examples and use cases that demonstrate their capabilities. By mastering these tools, you will enhance your data processing skills and significantly increase your efficiency in working with data, ultimately leading to more informed decision-making.

Choosing the Right Library for Your Task in python

In the ever-evolving landscape of Python programming, the abundance of libraries available can be both a boon and a curse. With thousands of libraries catering to various needs, it can be daunting to choose the right one for your specific task. This chapter aims to guide you through the decision-making process, helping you identify the most suitable libraries based on your project's requirements.

Understanding the Task at Hand

Before delving into specific libraries, it's crucial to have a clear understanding of the task you are trying to accomplish. Python is a versatile language used in diverse fields such as web development, data analysis, machine learning, scientific computing, automation, and more. Here are some key considerations you should evaluate:

Define the Problem: Clearly articulate what problem you are trying to solve. Having a well-defined problem statement can help narrow down your library choices.

Outcomes and Goals: What specific outcomes are you hoping to achieve? Do you need to process data, create visualizations, or build a web application? Recognizing your end goals will assist in selecting appropriate tools.

Performance Requirements: Consider the efficiency of your solution. Some tasks may require high performance, while others may prioritize ease of use or flexibility.

Complexity and Learning Curve: Assess how complex the library is and whether it aligns with your current skill level. It's essential to choose a library that you can effectively learn and utilize without overwhelming yourself.

Categories of Libraries

Python libraries can be categorized based on their functionality. Here are some common categories along with examples and considerations for selection:

1. **Data Manipulation and Analysis**

For tasks involving data manipulation, libraries such as **Pandas** and **NumPy** are essential.

Pandas: Ideal for data wrangling and analysis, it provides high-level data structures and functions needed to work with structured data.

NumPy: A fundamental package for scientific computing, NumPy offers support for large arrays and matrices, along with mathematical functions to operate on them.

Considerations: Use these libraries for tasks involving large datasets and complex numerical computations. The choice between them often depends on whether you require data manipulation (Pandas) or fast numerical operations (NumPy).

2. **Data Visualization**

When it comes to visualizing data, the selection varies based on the type of visualization and complexity you need:

Matplotlib: A foundational plotting library for creating static, animated, and interactive visualizations in Python.

Seaborn: Built on top of Matplotlib, Seaborn simplifies many plotting tasks and can create more visually appealing statistical plots with less code.

Plotly: Ideal for creating interactive charts and dashboards, especially for web applications.

Considerations: Choose Matplotlib for basic visualizations, Seaborn for statistical visuals, and Plotly for interactive plots.

3. **Machine Learning and AI**

For machine learning tasks, several libraries stand out:

Scikit-learn: A versatile library for traditional machine learning algorithms. It's user-friendly and great for beginners.

TensorFlow and **PyTorch**: These libraries are preferred for deep learning and neural networks. They support building and training complex models.

Considerations: Start with Scikit-learn for simpler tasks, and opt for TensorFlow or PyTorch when working with deep learning models.

4. **Web Development**

When building web applications, the choice of library or framework can significantly impact your development process:

Flask: A micro-framework that allows for flexibility and simplicity, ideal for small applications or microservices.

Django: A high-level web framework that promotes rapid development and clean design, suitable for larger applications.

Considerations: Choose Flask for small projects requiring quick setup and Django for larger applications needing robust features like authentication and an admin panel.

5. **Automation and Scripting**

For task automation, the built-in libraries and frameworks available in Python can simplify workflows:

Requests: Perfect for making HTTP requests easily, useful for APIs and web interactions.

Beautiful Soup: A library for parsing HTML and XML documents; great for web scraping tasks.

Selenium: An automated testing framework that can also be used for web scraping, capable of controlling web browsers programmatically.

Considerations: Use Requests for API interactions, Beautiful Soup for scraping static pages, and Selenium when JavaScript is involved.

Community and Documentation

It's important to assess the community support and quality of documentation available for a library. Libraries with active communities often have extensive resources such as tutorials, forums, and GitHub repositories.

Moreover, well-documented libraries facilitate faster learning curves and smoother troubleshooting processes.

With the right approach and a clear understanding of your needs, you can select libraries that not only make your development process smoother but also enhance the efficiency and quality of the solutions you build. As you continue on your Python journey, remember to stay updated with new libraries and advancements in the ecosystem to always equip yourself with the best tools for the job.

Chapter 5: Python Scripts for Excel Tasks

Whether for data analysis, reporting, or automating repetitive tasks, being able to manipulate Excel files programmatically can save time, reduce errors, and enhance productivity. In this chapter, we will explore how to utilize Python scripts to handle various Excel tasks efficiently.

5.1 Introduction to Python and Excel

Python, with its rich ecosystem of libraries, is a powerful tool for data manipulation. Among these libraries,

`pandas` and `openpyxl` are particularly useful when dealing with Excel files. `pandas` offers flexible data structures and data analysis tools, while `openpyxl` allows for reading and writing Excel 2010 xlsx/xlsm/xltx/xltm files. Understanding how to leverage these libraries opens the door to effectively handling a wide range of Excel-related tasks.

Why Use Python for Excel?

Automation: Automating repetitive tasks such as data entry, calculations, and reporting can save hours of manual work.

Data Analysis: Python's data manipulation capabilities are far superior to what Excel can offer, especially for large datasets.

Integration: Combining data from Excel with other data sources becomes straightforward, enabling more comprehensive analyses.

5.2 Setting Up the Environment

Before diving into writing Python scripts, ensure you have the necessary environment set up.

Installation: First, make sure you have Python installed on your machine. You can download it from [python.org](https://www.python.org/downloads/). It is advisable to use a package manager like `conda` or `pip` to install required libraries.

```bash
pip install pandas openpyxl
```

IDE: To write and execute your scripts, an Integrated Development Environment (IDE) such as Jupyter Notebook, PyCharm, or Visual Studio Code can be utilized.

5.3 Reading Excel Files with Pandas

One of the first tasks you'll often want to perform is reading data from an Excel file. The `pandas` library simplifies this process significantly.

Example: Reading an Excel File

```python
import pandas as pd
# Load the Excel file file_path = 'data.xlsx'
df = pd.read_excel(file_path, sheet_name='Sheet1')
```

```python
# Display the first few rows of the dataframe
print(df.head())
```

In this example, we used the `read_excel` function to load an Excel sheet into a DataFrame. The `head()` method allows us to preview the first few rows of the data, which is useful for understanding its structure.

5.4 Writing Data to Excel Files

Once you have manipulated or analyzed your data, you will likely want to write the results back to an Excel file. This can also be done seamlessly with `pandas`.

Example: Writing to an Excel File

```python
# Modify DataFrame (e.g., adding a new column) df['New Column'] = df['Existing Column'] * 2

# Save the modified DataFrame to a new Excel file output_path = 'modified_data.xlsx' df.to_excel(output_path, index=False)
```

In this example, we created a new column by performing a basic arithmetic operation, then wrote the modified DataFrame to a new Excel file. The `index=False` argument ensures that the DataFrame's index is not written into the Excel sheet.

5.5 Automating Excel Reports

One of the common use cases for automating Excel tasks is generating reports. Using Python, you can create scripts that compile data, perform analyses, and format the report in Excel.

Example: Generating a Simple Report

```python
# Function to generate a report def generate_report(dataframe):

summary = dataframe.describe()  # Get a statistical summary summary.to_excel('report_summary.xlsx')  # Save the summary as an Excel file

# Generate the report based on the DataFrame generate_report(df)
```

With the `describe()` function, we provide a statistical summary of the DataFrame and save this summary as a new Excel file for easier sharing and reporting.

5.6 Dealing with Multiple Sheets

Many Excel files contain multiple sheets. Python scripts can easily handle reading from and writing to multiple sheets, allowing for comprehensive data management.

Example: Reading and Writing Multiple Sheets

```python
# Reading multiple sheets xls = pd.ExcelFile(file_path)

df1 = pd.read_excel(xls, sheet_name='Sheet1') df2 = pd.read_excel(xls, sheet_name='Sheet2')

# Writing to multiple sheets

with pd.ExcelWriter('multiples_sheets.xlsx') as writer:
```

```
df1.to_excel(writer,          sheet_name='Summary',
index=False) df2.to_excel(writer, sheet_name='Details',
index=False)
```
` ` `

In this example, we read multiple sheets and then wrote them back into a new Excel file with a specified sheet structure.

Python provides an array of functionalities for working with Excel, making it an invaluable skill for data professionals. By mastering the techniques discussed in this chapter—reading from and writing to Excel files, automating reports, and handling multiple sheets—you will be equipped to streamline your Excel- related tasks significantly.

Reading and Writing Excel Files in python

As data continues to play a pivotal role in decision-making processes across various industries, knowing how to effectively manipulate data is crucial. Among the numerous data formats available, Microsoft Excel remains a popular choice due to its user-friendly interface and powerful functionalities. Fortunately, Python, a versatile programming language, offers robust libraries that allow you to read from and write to Excel files effortlessly. In this chapter, we will explore how to work with Excel files using Python, primarily focusing on two libraries: `pandas` and `openpyxl`.

Why Use Excel with Python?

Excel files are ubiquitous in data management, finance, data analysis, and reporting tasks. Using Python to interact with these files can provide significant advantages:

Automation: Automate repetitive tasks such as data cleaning, reports generation, and more.

Data Analysis: Leverage Python's powerful data analysis libraries alongside Excel, allowing for more complex manipulations and visualizations.

Integration: Easily integrate with web applications and databases for more extensive data workflows. ## Libraries for Reading and Writing Excel Files

1. Pandas

Pandas is an open-source data analysis and manipulation library for Python that provides extensive support for working with structured data, including Excel files.

Installation

First, ensure you have the `pandas` and `openpyxl` libraries installed:

```bash
pip install pandas openpyxl
```

Reading Excel Files with Pandas

To read an Excel file, use the `read_excel` function provided by the `pandas` library. Here's a simple example:

```python
```

77

```python
import pandas as pd

# Read an Excel file  file_path = 'sample_data.xlsx' df =
pd.read_excel(file_path)

# Display the DataFrame print(df.head())
```

The above code snippet will read the first sheet of the
specified `Excel` file and return a pandas DataFrame
containing the data.

Specifying Sheet Names

If your Excel file contains multiple sheets, you can specify
which sheet to read by using the `sheet_name`
parameter:

```python
# Read a specific sheet

df = pd.read_excel(file_path, sheet_name='Sheet1')

# Display the DataFrame print(df)
```

Writing Data to Excel Files

Writing to an Excel file is just as simple. You can create a
new Excel file or add data to an existing one. Here's how
to create a new Excel file:

```python
# Create a new DataFrame data = {

'Name': ['Alice', 'Bob', 'Charlie'], 'Age': [25, 30, 35],
```

```
'City': ['New York', 'Los Angeles', 'Chicago']
}
new_df = pd.DataFrame(data)
# Write the DataFrame to an Excel file
new_df.to_excel('output_data.xlsx', index=False)
```

In this example, we define a new DataFrame and then write it to `output_data.xlsx`. The `index=False` argument prevents pandas from writing the DataFrame index as a column in the Excel file.

2. OpenPyXL

While `pandas` provides high-level access to Excel files, `openpyxl` allows for more intricate manipulations and is an excellent tool for tasks requiring fine control over Excel's features.

Installation

To use `openpyxl`, install it using pip:

```bash
pip install openpyxl
```

Reading Excel Files with OpenPyXL

Here's how to read data from an Excel file using `openpyxl`:

```python
from openpyxl import load_workbook
```

```python
# Load the workbook
workbook = load_workbook('sample_data.xlsx') sheet = workbook.active

# Read data from specific cells
for row in sheet.iter_rows(values_only=True):
print(row)
```

The above example opens an Excel file and iterates over each row, printing the values. #### Writing Data to Excel Files with OpenPyXL

You can also write data to an Excel file using `openpyxl`. Here's an example:

```python
from openpyxl import Workbook

# Create a new workbook and activate it new_workbook = Workbook() new_sheet = new_workbook.active

# Adding data to the sheet new_sheet['A1'] = 'Name' new_sheet['B1'] = 'Age'

# Iterate to add more data data = [
('Alice', 25),
('Bob', 30),
('Charlie', 35)
]
for name, age in data:
new_sheet.append([name, age])
```

```
# Save the workbook
new_workbook.save('output_openpyxl.xlsx')
```

This example demonstrates how to create a new Excel workbook, write column headers, and append rows of data before saving the file.

In this chapter, we covered how to read and write Excel files in Python using the `pandas` and `openpyxl` libraries. Understanding these libraries equips you with the tools necessary to automate data handling tasks and integrate Excel with powerful Python applications. As you continue your journey in data analysis and manipulation, mastering Excel file operations in Python will undoubtedly enhance your capabilities and streamline your workflows.

Manipulating Data with Python

Enter Python—a versatile programming language that offers a range of libraries specifically designed for data manipulation and analysis, including working with Excel files. In this chapter, we will explore some of the fundamental techniques for manipulating Excel data using Python, focusing on popular libraries such as

`Pandas` and `openpyxl`.

Why Use Python for Excel Manipulation?

The advantages of using Python to manipulate Excel data are numerous:

Automation: Python scripts can automate repetitive tasks, saving time and reducing the likelihood of errors.

81

Scalability: Python can handle larger datasets than Excel typically can, thanks to its powerful libraries.

Complex Analysis: With Python, you can easily apply complex mathematical operations and integrate with machine learning libraries.

Reproducibility: Python scripts can be easily shared and executed, creating reproducible data analysis workflows.

Setting Up Your Environment

Before we dive into manipulating Excel data, we need to set up our Python environment. For this, we will utilize the following libraries:

Pandas: A powerful data manipulation and analysis library.

OpenPyXL: A library for reading and writing Excel files in `.xlsx` format. ### Installing Required Libraries

You can easily install these libraries using `pip`:

```bash
pip install pandas openpyxl
```

Basic Operations with Pandas ### Loading Excel Files

The first step in data manipulation is to load the data from an Excel file. With Pandas, this can be achieved using the `read_excel()` function.

```python
import pandas as pd
```

```python
# Load an Excel file
df = pd.read_excel('path_to_your_file.xlsx', sheet_name='Sheet1')
```

Exploring the Data

Once the data is loaded into a DataFrame, you can begin to explore it:

```python
# Display the first five rows print(df.head())

# Get basic statistics print(df.describe())

# Check for missing values print(df.isnull().sum())
```

Data Cleaning

Data cleaning is a crucial step in data analysis. You may need to remove duplicates, fill missing values, or change data types.

```python
# Remove duplicates df.drop_duplicates(inplace=True)

# Fill missing values df.fillna(0, inplace=True)

# Change a column's data type df['Date'] = pd.to_datetime(df['Date'])
```

Data Manipulation

Data manipulation may involve filtering rows, selecting specific columns, or performing operations on the data.

83

Filtering Data

You can filter rows in a DataFrame based on specific conditions:

```python
# Filter rows where the value in 'Amount' is greater than
100 filtered_df = df[df['Amount'] > 100]
```

Selecting Columns

Selecting specific columns is straightforward:

```python
# Select 'Date' and 'Amount' columns selected_df =
df[['Date', 'Amount']]
```

Grouping Data

Pandas allows you to group data and perform aggregate functions for analysis:

```python
# Group by 'Category' and calculate the sum of 'Amount'
grouped_df = df.groupby('Category')['Amount'].sum()
print(grouped_df)
```

Writing to Excel

After manipulation, you may want to save your results back to an Excel file. This can be done using the `to_excel()` function.

```python
# Write the DataFrame to a new Excel file
df.to_excel('output_file.xlsx', index=False)
```

Advanced Excel Manipulation with OpenPyXL

While Pandas is great for data manipulation, OpenPyXL allows for more advanced operations, such as modifying existing Excel files including formatting and styling.

Opening an Existing Workbook

```python
from openpyxl import load_workbook

# Load an existing workbook

workbook = load_workbook('path_to_your_file.xlsx')
sheet = workbook.active
```

Reading Cell Values

You can read and write individual cell values with OpenPyXL:

```python
# Read a specific cell value cell_value = sheet['A1'].value
print(cell_value)

# Write a new value to a cell sheet['B1'] = 'New Value'
```

Formatting Cells

OpenPyXL enables you to format cells for improved

readability. For example, you can change font styles or add colors:

```python
from openpyxl.styles import Font, Color

# Change font style
sheet['A1'].font = Font(bold=True, color='FF0000')  # Red bold text
```

Saving Changes

After making changes, don't forget to save your workbook:

```python
# Save the workbook workbook.save('modified_file.xlsx')
```

In this chapter, we have covered the basics of manipulating data in Excel using Python. We have seen how to read, explore, clean, manipulate, and write Excel files using the Pandas and OpenPyXL libraries. These tools provide powerful capabilities to automate and improve your data workflows beyond the manual capabilities of Excel. The next chapter will delve into more complex data analysis techniques, leveraging the power of Python to derive insights from your datasets.

Chapter 6: Advanced Python Techniques for Excel

However, integrating the power of Python with Excel can elevate your productivity, streamline your processes, and unlock advanced analytical capabilities. This chapter delves into advanced Python techniques for working with Excel files, enabling you to automate tasks, analyze data more effectively, and leverage the full potential of both technologies.

6.1 Using Pandas for Advanced Data Analysis

Pandas is an open-source library designed for data manipulation and analysis. It provides data structures like Series and DataFrames, which facilitate easy handling of data from Excel files. Utilizing Pandas, we can read from and write to Excel files, as well as perform complex operations like filtering, grouping, and aggregating data.

6.1.1 Reading Excel Files

You can read Excel files using the `read_excel` function from Pandas. For example:

```python
import pandas as pd

# Load an Excel file

df = pd.read_excel('data.xlsx', sheet_name='Sheet1')
print(df.head())
```

6.1.2 Writing Data to Excel

You can also write data back to Excel, either modifying an

existing file or creating a new one:

```python
# Write DataFrame to Excel
df.to_excel('output.xlsx',          sheet_name='Results',
index=False)
```

6.1.3 Data Manipulation Techniques

With Pandas, you can perform various operations, such as:

- **Filtering Data**: Select rows based on conditions:

```python
filtered_df = df[df['Column1'] > 100]
```

- **Grouping Data**: Aggregate data based on certain criteria:

```python
grouped_df = df.groupby('Category').sum()
```

- **Merging and Joining**: Combine multiple DataFrames:

```python
merged_df = pd.merge(df1, df2, on='ID', how='inner')
```

6.2 Automating Excel with OpenPyXL

For more advanced control over Excel files, `openpyxl` is an excellent library, especially when you want to manage elements such as formatting, charts, or even formulas.

6.2.1 Creating and Modifying Excel Files

Using OpenPyXL, you can create and modify Excel documents programmatically:

```python
from openpyxl import Workbook

# Create a new workbook and select the active sheet wb =
Workbook()

ws = wb.active

# Add data

ws['A1'] = 'Sample Data' ws['A2'] = 42

# Save the workbook wb.save('new_file.xlsx')
```

6.2.2 Formatting Cells

OpenPyXL allows you to apply styles and formats to cells:

```python
from openpyxl.styles import Font, Color

ws['A1'].font = Font(bold=True, color='FF0000')  # Red
bold font
```

```
```

6.2.3 Adding Charts

Visual representation is key in any data analysis. With OpenPyXL, you can create charts directly:

```python
from openpyxl.chart import BarChart, Reference

chart = BarChart()

data = Reference(ws, min_col=1, min_row=1, max_col=1, max_row=10)                            chart.add_data(data, titles_from_data=True)

ws.add_chart(chart, "E5")
```

6.3 Excel Integration with Automation Libraries

Python provides powerful libraries such as `pyautogui` and `win32com` for automating Excel tasks even further. These libraries can interact with Excel as if a user were manually performing the operations.

6.3.1 Automating Tasks with `pyautogui`

`pyautogui` enables mouse and keyboard automation. This is particularly useful for repetitive tasks in Excel:

```python
import pyautogui

# Example: Open Excel and perform some basic navigation pyautogui.hotkey('ctrl', 'o') # Opens the file dialog
```

```
```

6.3.2 Using `win32com` for More Control

For Windows users, the `win32com` library allows direct interactions with Excel through its COM interface:

```python
import win32com.client

# Launch an instance of Excel

excel = win32com.client.Dispatch('Excel.Application')
excel.Visible = True

# Open a workbook

workbook = excel.Workbooks.Open('C:\\path\\to\\file.xlsx') sheet = workbook.Sheets(1)

value = sheet.Cells(1, 1).Value # Read from A1
workbook.Close(SaveChanges=False)
```

6.4 Advanced Excel Functions via Python

By combining Python with Excel's built-in functions, you can create dynamic and powerful analyses. For instance, implementing statistical analyses using libraries like `scipy` or `statsmodels` can further enhance your Excel functionalities.

6.4.1 Custom Formulas in Excel

Using Python, you can define and insert custom formulas into your Excel sheets:

```python
```

```python
ws['B1'] = '=SUM(A1:A10)'  # Insert Excel formula
```

6.4.2 Running Statistical Analysis

You can perform advanced statistical calculations in Python and then export the results to Excel:

```python
from scipy import stats

# Sample data
data = [1, 2, 3, 4, 5]
mean = stats.tmean(data)
ws['C1'] = mean  # Insert result into Excel
```

By utilizing libraries like Pandas, OpenPyXL, and automation tools such as `win32com`, you can automate repetitive tasks, conduct complex analyses, and create dynamic reports with ease. As we continue to explore Python's expansive capabilities, these advanced techniques will serve as the foundation for optimizing your Excel workflows. Whether you're managing large datasets, generating complex financial models, or simply striving for efficiency, these tools empower you to unlock an entirely new level of productivity.

Handling Complex Data Structures

While most users are familiar with handling simple

datasets consisting of rows and columns, Excel also possesses powerful capabilities for working with complex data structures. In this chapter, we will explore how to manage these intricate data arrangements, including nested tables, hierarchical data, and multi- dimensional arrays. Understanding how to effectively handle these structures is crucial for making informed decisions based on sophisticated datasets.

Understanding Complex Data Structures ### 1. Defining Complex Data Structures

Complex data structures in Excel go beyond basic tabular data and can include combinations of tables, lists, arrays, and objects. Examples include:

Nested Tables: Tables within tables that represent multi-level relationships.

Hierarchical Data: Data that is organized into a parent-child relationship, such as organizational charts or product categories.

Multi-Dimensional Arrays: Data that spans across multiple dimensions, often seen in financial modeling or data cubes.

2. Recognizing the Need for Complexity

Simple datasets can often lead to oversights or misinterpretations. Complex data structures allow for more nuanced data representation, aiding in the analysis of trends, correlations, and patterns that would be difficult to discern in a flat file. Examples of when to utilize complex structures include:

Inventory Management: Managing stocks that are organized by category, sub-category, and supplier.

Sales Data: Analyzing performance across multiple regions, products, and time frames.

Project Management: Tracking tasks that have dependencies, resources, and timelines. ## Techniques for Handling Complex Data Structures

1. Using Excel Tables

Excel Tables are an effective way to manage complex datasets. They allow for dynamic data ranges, facilitating easier data manipulation and analysis. Key features include:

Structured References: Creating formulas that reference table fields by name, improving clarity.

Auto Expansion: Tables automatically expand as new rows are added.

Sorting and Filtering: Built-in features that help in organizing and analyzing data quickly.

Example: Create a nested table to represent product categories. Each category can have multiple products, each with its attributes and sales figures.

2. Implementing Data Validation and Drop-down Lists

Data validation helps maintain data integrity within complex structures. By implementing drop-down lists, users can easily select from pre-defined options, which minimizes the risk of errors.

Steps to Create a Drop-down List:

Select the cell where the drop-down needs to be created.

Go to the **Data** tab and click on **Data Validation**.

In the dialog box, set the validation criteria to "List" and provide the source range.

Click **OK** to create the drop-down list. ### 3. Utilizing PivotTables

PivotTables are a powerful feature for summarizing and analyzing complex datasets. They enable users to dynamically reorganize and manipulate data to uncover insights.

Creating a PivotTable:

Select the dataset and navigate to the **Insert** tab.

Click **PivotTable** and choose where to place the PivotTable.

Drag fields into the Rows, Columns, Values, and Filters areas to customize the view. ### 4. Navigating Hierarchical Structures

Managing hierarchical data often requires specialized techniques. One effective way to handle this is through the use of outlining and grouping features.

Grouping: Select rows or columns and right-click to group, creating a collapsible outline.

Use of Indents: Indent rows to signify hierarchy, improving readability.

Example: Use grouping to create an organizational chart in Excel, where each department can be collapsed or expanded as needed.

Advanced Tools for Complex Data Structures ### 1. Using Power Query

Power Query is a powerful tool for importing and

transforming complex data from various sources. It can handle large volumes of data and perform advanced data manipulations.

Steps to Use Power Query:

Navigate to the **Data** tab and select **Get & Transform Data**.

Choose your data source and use the Power Query Editor to clean and shape the data.

Load the transformed data into Excel for analysis. ### 2. Incorporating VBA for Automation

Visual Basic for Applications (VBA) enables users to automate repetitive tasks in managing complex data structures. By writing scripts, users can save time and reduce errors associated with manual data handling.

Example of a Simple VBA Script:

```vba
Sub AutoFillComplexStructure() Dim ws As Worksheet

Set ws = ThisWorkbook.Sheets("Data")

With ws

' Automatically fill down a series in a specified range

.Range("A1:A10").FillDown End With

End Sub
```

By utilizing tables, data validation, PivotTables, Power Query, and VBA, users can transform vast arrays of data into actionable insights. As we progress further into an era defined by data, mastering these skills will be invaluable for professionals across all sectors. In the following chapters, we will delve deeper into specific case studies and practical applications of complex data handling in Excel, enabling readers to apply what they have learned in real-world scenarios.

Optimizing Python Scripts for Performance in Excel

The integration of Python with Excel allows users to leverage powerful data processing capabilities that are not readily available through Excel's native formulas and functions. However, as scripts grow in complexity and data size increases, performance optimization becomes a crucial consideration. This chapter aims to provide strategies for optimizing Python scripts to improve performance when working with Excel data.

Understanding the Bottlenecks

Before diving into optimization techniques, it's essential to understand where performance bottlenecks might occur. Common bottlenecks in Python scripts interacting with Excel include:

I/O Operations: Reading from or writing to Excel files can be slow, especially for large datasets.

Data Processing: Inefficient algorithms and data handling can significantly slow down execution time.

Memory Usage: Excessive memory consumption can lead to swapping and overall sluggishness of the system.

By identifying these bottlenecks, programmers can focus

99

their optimization efforts more effectively. ## Choosing the Right Libraries

The choice of libraries can have a significant impact on performance. Some popular libraries for handling Excel files and data manipulations include:

Pandas: Excellent for data manipulation but can be slow when operating directly with Excel files.

OpenPyXL: Suitable for reading and writing Excel files. It's great for quick tasks but less efficient for large data manipulations.

XlsxWriter: Optimized for writing Excel files, it can efficiently create complex Excel files with formats.

Optimization often begins with choosing the right library for the specific task at hand. ## Loading Data Efficiently

Loading data efficiently is one of the first steps in optimizing your script. Here are some strategies to consider:

Use `read_excel` with Relevant Parameters: When using Pandas, specify relevant parameters such as `usecols` to only load the necessary columns and `skiprows` to bypass unneeded rows.

```python
import pandas as pd

df = pd.read_excel('data.xlsx', usecols='A:C', skiprows=5)
```

Limit the Data Size Early: If you know you only need a specific subset of a large dataset, filter it right at the loading stage to reduce the amount of data in memory.

Consider Data Formats: If working with very large files, consider converting the Excel file to a more efficient format like CSV or Parquet for quicker I/O operations.

Data Manipulation Techniques

Efficiently manipulating data can greatly enhance performance. Here are some techniques:

Vectorization: Leverage the power of vectorized operations in Pandas instead of looping through DataFrame rows. This can provide significant speed improvements.

```python
df['new_column'] = df['column1'] + df['column2']
```

Avoiding Loops: Avoid explicit loops in favor of built-in functions which are optimized for performance. For example, using `apply()` can be slower than using built-in functions.

Batch Processing: For very large datasets that need multiple transformations, consider breaking them into smaller chunks and processing each chunk independently.

Caching Results

Repeatedly computing the same results can be costly. Caching can help enhance performance in such cases:

Using Intermediary Files: Save intermediate results to disk, so they don't need to be recomputed.

```python df.to_pickle('intermediate_results.pkl')
```

```
```

Memoization: For functions that are computationally heavy and called multiple times, consider implementing memoization to store previously computed results.

Optimizing Output

When outputting data to Excel, efficiency is key, especially with large datasets:

Batch Write Operations: Instead of writing each individual piece of data to the Excel file, compile your results into a single DataFrame and write it all at once.

```python
df.to_excel('output.xlsx', index=False)
```

Limit Formats: When writing to Excel, limit additional formatting as it can slow down the saving process significantly.

Use Efficient Libraries: Leverage libraries that are optimized for writing large amounts of data, such as XlsxWriter, which can handle larger data sets more efficiently than OpenPyXL.

Profiling and Benchmarking

To effectively optimize, it's important to measure the performance of your scripts. You can use:

cProfile: A built-in Python module to profile your code and identify bottlenecks.

Line Profiler: A tool to measure the time spent on each individual line of code.

Use these tools to benchmark before and after optimizations to see the efficacy of your changes. ## Conclusion

Optimizing Python scripts for performance when dealing with Excel data is a multifaceted process that involves understanding bottlenecks, choosing the right libraries, utilizing efficient data manipulation techniques, and strategically managing output. By implementing these strategies, data analysts and engineers can significantly enhance the speed and efficiency of their Python scripts, ultimately leading to a smoother and more productive workflow.

Further Reading

"Python for Data Analysis" by Wes McKinney

"Effective Python: 90 Specific Ways to Write Better Python" by Brett Slatkin

As data requirements continue to grow, the optimization of code will remain an essential skill for Python developers working in the Excel ecosystem. Through careful consideration and application of the techniques outlined in this chapter, you can harness the full potential of Python while maintaining optimum performance in your data handling tasks.

Chapter 7: Integrating Python with Excel User Forms

While Microsoft Excel remains one of the most popular tools for data management, enhancing its functionality with Python can provide significant benefits. In this chapter, we will explore how to integrate Python with Excel using user forms to create interactive applications that streamline data entry, improve accuracy, and enhance user experience.

7.1 Understanding Excel User Forms

Excel User Forms are custom dialog boxes that allow users to interact with the data in a more controlled and user-friendly manner. They can be used to capture user input, display data, and navigate between different sections of a workbook. User Forms offer several advantages:

Guided Input: Users can enter data into structured fields designed to minimize errors.

Visual Appeal: Forms can enhance user engagement with visual elements like labels, drop-down lists, and buttons.

Data Validation: Input can be validated in real time, ensuring that the data entering the system is accurate and complete.

Python can be utilized to automate the creation, management, and manipulation of these User Forms, allowing for a seamless integration of Python scripts and Excel functionalities.

7.2 Setting Up the Environment

Before diving into coding, it is essential to set up the environment. You will need the following:

Microsoft Excel: Ensure you have a version of Excel that supports VBA (Visual Basic for Applications).

Python: Install Python (preferably version 3.x).

Libraries: Install libraries such as `openpyxl`, `pandas`, and `xlwings`. The `xlwings` library is particularly useful as it creates seamless integrations between Python and Excel.

```bash
pip install openpyxl pandas xlwings
```

7.3 Creating a Basic User Form in Excel

Open Excel and create a new workbook.

Access the Developer Tab: If the Developer tab is not visible, enable it by going to `File > Options > Customize Ribbon` and checking the Developer option.

Insert a User Form: In the Developer tab, click on "Insert" and choose "User Form."

Design the Form: Use the toolbox to add various controls like Text Boxes, Labels, Combo Boxes, and Command Buttons.

For instance, create a form to capture customer information with fields for name, email, phone number, and a button to submit the data.

7.4 Programming the User Form with VBA

Once your User Form is ready, it's time to add some VBA code to handle user interactions. For instance, to add data validation or a command button to submit the form, follow these steps:

Double-click the Command Button to open the code editor.

Write a simple script that captures user input and writes it to a spreadsheet:

```vba
Private Sub btnSubmit_Click() Dim ws As Worksheet

Set ws = ThisWorkbook.Sheets("CustomerData")

ws.Range("A1").End(xlDown).Offset(1, 0).Value = txtName.Value  ws.Range("B1").End(xlDown).Offset(1, 0).Value = txtEmail.Value  ws.Range("C1").End(xlDown).Offset(1, 0).Value = txtPhone.Value

' Clear the form fields txtName.Value = "" txtEmail.Value = "" txtPhone.Value = ""

MsgBox "Data Submitted Successfully!" End Sub
```

7.5 Connecting Python to Excel

Now that the User Form is built and programmed, you can connect it to Python to manipulate the data further or automate processes. Here, `xlwings` serves as a crucial bridge between Excel and Python.

Use `xlwings` to Launch the Excel Application:

```python
```

```python
import xlwings as xw

def launch_excel():

wb = xw.Book('path_to_your_file.xlsx')  # Replace with your Excel file path xw.apps[0].visible = True  # Make Excel visible

return wb
```

Read Data: You can read the entered data into Python for further processing:

```python
def read_customer_data(wb):

sheet = wb.sheets['CustomerData']  data = sheet.range('A1').expand().value

print(data)  # Display the data in the console
```

Write Data: You can also write data back to the User Form or to another worksheet.

```python
def write_data_to_excel(wb, customer_info):  sheet = wb.sheets['CustomerData']


next_row = sheet.range('A1').end('down').row + 1


sheet.range(f'A{next_row}').value = customer_info['name'] sheet.range(f'B{next_row}').value = customer_info['email']
```

```
sheet.range(f'C{next_row}').value        =
customer_info['phone']
```

7.6 Error Handling and Validation

When integrating Python with Excel, it's essential to handle errors and ensure validation checks are in place. Use try-except blocks in Python to catch potential issues:

```python
python try:
launch_excel() except Exception as e:

print(f"An error occurred: {e}")
```

Additionally, implement validations in both Excel and Python to ensure data integrity. For instance, a user's email should conform to a valid email format.

7.7 Real-world Applications

Integrating Python with Excel User Forms opens the door to various practical applications:

Data Collection Tools: Build tools for survey data collection that automatically log responses to Excel.

Inventory Management: Create user forms to manage inventory systems that update stock levels directly from user inputs.

Reporting Dashboards: Combine user forms to gather parameters from users and generate custom reports based on those inputs.

Integrating Python with Excel User Forms bridges the gap between simple data entry and complex data manipulation, allowing users to harness the power of Python's extensive libraries while benefiting from Excel's familiarity and ease of use. By following the steps outlined in this chapter, you can build interactive applications that enhance user engagement, improve accuracy, and provide powerful insights into your data.

Creating and Customizing User Forms in Excel with Python

Leveraging the functionality of Excel through Python can significantly enhance the capability to manipulate data, generate reports, and streamline workflows. This chapter aims to guide you through creating and customizing user forms in Excel using Python, specifically with the help of libraries such as `openpyxl`,

`tkinter`, and `pandas`.

1. Understanding User Forms in Excel

User forms are an intuitive way to gather data from users in a structured format. They allow users to enter information directly into the spreadsheet without navigating through the cells, ensuring data accuracy and integrity. User forms can include text boxes, drop-down lists, checkboxes, and buttons, providing flexibility in data collection.

1.1 Why Use Python?

Python has become one of the most popular programming languages in the world, not only due to its simplicity but also its power in handling data. By using Python to create user forms in Excel, users can automate processes, validate inputs, and manage data more efficiently.

2. Setting Up Your Environment

To get started, you'll need to ensure your environment is set up correctly:

2.1 Install Required Libraries

You will need the following Python libraries:

111

`openpyxl` for reading and writing Excel files.

`tkinter` for creating graphical user interfaces (GUIs).

`pandas` for data manipulation and analysis. Install them using pip:

```bash
pip install openpyxl pandas
```

2.2 Setting Up Excel File

Create a new Excel file (.xlsx) where the user form data will be saved. For demonstration, we'll refer to it as `user_data.xlsx`.

3. Creating a Basic User Form

Now that your environment is set up, let's create a basic user form using `tkinter` and connect it to Excel using `openpyxl`.

3.1 Designing the User Form with Tkinter

Here's a simple example of a user form that collects a user's name and age:

```python
import tkinter as tk
from openpyxl import Workbook
def save_data():
name = entry_name.get() age = entry_age.get()
```

```python
# Create or load the workbook try:
wb = Workbook('user_data.xlsx') sheet = wb.active
# Write headers if this is a new file if sheet.max_row == 1:
sheet.append(["Name", "Age"]) # Append data to the
worksheet          sheet.append([name,          age])
wb.save('user_data.xlsx')
lbl_result.config(text="Data saved successfully!") except
Exception as e:
lbl_result.config(text=f"Error: {str(e)}")
# Setting up the Tkinter window root = tk.Tk()
root.title("User Data Entry Form")
# Creating the form fields
lbl_name  =  tk.Label(root, text="Enter your Name:")
lbl_name.pack()
entry_name = tk.Entry(root) entry_name.pack()
lbl_age  =  tk.Label(root,  text="Enter  your  Age:")
lbl_age.pack()
entry_age = tk.Entry(root) entry_age.pack()
btn_submit    =    tk.Button(root,    text="Submit",
command=save_data) btn_submit.pack()
lbl_result   =   tk.Label(root,   text="",   fg="green")
lbl_result.pack()
# Running the Tkinter event loop root.mainloop()
```

Explanation of the Code

Creating the Form: The `tkinter` library is used to create the main window and label, entry, and button widgets.

Saving Data: The `save_data()` function retrieves the data entered into the form and saves it to the

`user_data.xlsx` file using `openpyxl`.

Feedback: A label `lbl_result` gives feedback to the user about the success or failure of the data saving operation.

4. Customizing the User Form

Once the basic user form is in place, the next step is to enhance its functionality and appearance. ### 4.1 Adding More Inputs

You can expand the form to include more data fields, such as email or address. Simply replicate the structure used for the name and age entries:

```python
lbl_email = tk.Label(root, text="Enter your Email:")
lbl_email.pack()

entry_email = tk.Entry(root) entry_email.pack()
```

4.2 Validating User Input

Input validation is crucial for maintaining data integrity. You can add checks in the `save_data()` function:

```python
```

114

```python
def save_data():
    name = entry_name.get() age = entry_age.get() email = entry_email.get()

    # Input validation

    if not name or not age or not email:
    lbl_result.config(text="All fields are required!", fg="red")
    return

    try:

    age = int(age)  # Checking if age is a number except ValueError:

    lbl_result.config(text="Age must be a number!", fg="red")
    return
```

4.3 Enhancing UI

To make the form visually appealing, you can use `tkinter` options for styling:

```python
root.config(bg="lightblue")
lbl_name.config(bg="lightblue")
entry_name.config(bg="white")

btn_submit.config(bg="green", fg="white")
```

Creating and customizing user forms in Excel with Python not only enhances the usability of your spreadsheets but also automates data collection processes efficiently. You learned the fundamental techniques to set up a basic user form and explored ways to expand its functionality and improve user experience.

In subsequent chapters, we will delve deeper into advanced form functionalities and integration techniques. For now, try experimenting with various inputs and validations to tailor the user forms to your specific data collection needs.

Linking Python Scripts to Excel Forms

With the pervasive use of spreadsheets in businesses, professional environments, and academic institutions, the ability to automate and enhance Excel tasks with powerful programming languages like Python opens up new avenues for efficiency and data management. This chapter aims to guide you through linking Python scripts to Excel forms, maximizing the functionality of your Excel files while integrating Python's robust data manipulation capabilities.

1. Understanding the Basics ### 1.1 What are Excel Forms?

Excel forms are user-friendly interfaces designed to enter, view, and manipulate data in Excel spreadsheets. They can be created with features like input prompts, dropdown menus, and checkboxes, allowing users to input and validate data without directly interacting with Excel tables.

1.2 Why Use Python with Excel?

Python is renowned for its readability and the vast ecosystem of libraries that simplify various programming tasks. Integrating Python with Excel can help:

Automate repetitive tasks

Analyze and visualize data more effectively

Process large datasets seamlessly

Perform complex calculations that Excel might struggle with ## 2. Setting Up the Environment

Before diving into linking Python scripts with Excel forms, ensure you have the right setup. ### 2.1 Required Libraries

To interact with Excel files using Python, you'll mainly need the following libraries:

Pandas: For data manipulation and analysis

OpenPyXL: For reading/writing Excel files

xlwings: A bridge to call Python from Excel, allowing real-time interaction

PyQt or Tkinter (optional): For creating custom forms in Python You can install these libraries using pip:

```bash

pip install pandas openpyxl xlwings

```

2.2 Excel Configuration

Create an Excel file and design your form using built-in Excel functionalities. Ensure that relevant input fields are clearly labeled, and apply data validation to maintain data integrity.

3. Connecting Python with Excel Forms

3.1 Reading Data from Excel to Python

Using Pandas, you can easily read data from your Excel forms:

```python
import pandas as pd
# Load the Excel file
df = pd.read_excel('path_to_file.xlsx', sheet_name='Sheet1')
# Displaying the DataFrame print(df)
```

3.2 Writing Data from Python to Excel

Once you process or analyze the data with Python, you can write data back into the Excel form:

```python
# Perform analysis or data manipulation on df
df['New_Column'] = df['Existing_Column'] * 2 # Example processing
# Save the modified DataFrame back to Excel
df.to_excel('path_to_file.xlsx', sheet_name='Sheet1', index=False)
```

3.3 Using xlwings for Real-Time Interaction

`xlwings` enables executing Python functions from Excel directly. Here's how to set it up:

In Excel, enable the xlwings Excel add-in.

Go to your Python script and define a function you want to call:

118

```python
import xlwings as xw
@xw.func
def calculate_total(a, b):
return a + b
```

In Excel, you can then call this function like a standard Excel formula:

```
=calculate_total(A1, B1)
```

3.4 Creating Custom Forms with Tkinter

For more advanced functionalities, you may create a custom GUI form using the Tkinter library, allowing for a tailored user experience. Below is a simple example of a form that collects user input and writes it back to an Excel file:

```python
import tkinter as tk
import pandas as pd
def submit():
name = entry_name.get() age = entry_age.get()

# Append data to Excel
df = pd.DataFrame({'Name': [name], 'Age': [age]})
```

```
df.to_excel('path_to_file.xlsx', mode='a', header=False,
index=False)
```

Creating the form root = tk.Tk()

```
root.title("Data Entry Form")
```

```
tk.Label(root, text="Name:").grid(row=0) tk.Label(root,
text="Age:").grid(row=1)
```

```
entry_name = tk.Entry(root) entry_age = tk.Entry(root)
```

```
entry_name.grid(row=0,                    column=1)
entry_age.grid(row=1, column=1)
```

```
tk.Button(root,                         text="Submit",
command=submit).grid(row=3,              column=0,
columnspan=2) root.mainloop()
```

```
` ` `
```

4. Best Practices

Error Handling: Always implement error handling in your scripts to manage unexpected user inputs and ensure data integrity.

Documentation: Comment and document your code thoroughly, especially when sharing it with non- technical users.

Data Validation: Use Excel's data validation features to restrict inputs to expected formats.

Backup Data: Regularly back up your Excel files to prevent data loss from unintentional overwrites.

Linking Python scripts to Excel forms creates a powerful synergy that can significantly enhance data handling capabilities. By leveraging libraries like Pandas,

OpenPyXL, and xlwings, you can automate processes, perform advanced analytics, and create intuitive data entry forms. As you explore further, consider combining more complex features within your Excel applications, such as data visualizations using Matplotlib or Seaborn, thereby elevating your data-driven decision-making processes.

Chapter 8: Automating Data Analysis with Python

Python, with its vast ecosystem of libraries and frameworks, has emerged as a powerful tool for automating data analysis tasks. This chapter explores how to leverage Python to develop automated data analysis workflows that enhance productivity and ensure consistency.

8.1 Introduction to Automation in Data Analysis

Automation refers to the process of using technology to perform tasks with minimal human intervention. In the realm of data analysis, automation can significantly reduce the time and effort required to collect, clean, analyze, and visualize data. By automating repetitive tasks, analysts can focus on the interpretation of results and strategic decision-making rather than getting bogged down in manual data processing.

8.1.1 Benefits of Automation

Efficiency: Automation speeds up data processing, allowing analysts and data scientists to work with larger datasets more effectively.

Consistency: Automated processes reduce the likelihood of human error, leading to more reliable and reproducible results.

Scalability: Automated procedures can easily be scaled to handle various data sizes, facilitating analysis as data volumes grow.

Focus on Insights: With routine tasks automated, data professionals can dedicate more time to deriving actionable insights from data.

8.2 Setting Up Your Python Environment

Before diving into automation, it's crucial to set up a proper Python environment. The following steps outline the process:

Install Python: Download and install the latest version of Python from the official website (python.org).

Package Management: Use `pip` to install essential libraries for data analysis:

```bash
pip install pandas numpy matplotlib seaborn scikit-learn jupyter
```

Jupyter Notebook: Jupyter Notebooks provide an interactive coding environment. Launch it by running:

```bash
jupyter notebook
```

Version Control: Introduce Git into your workflow for versioning and collaboration on data analysis scripts.

8.3 Data Collection Automation

Data collection is often the first step in any analysis workflow. Python's libraries can be used to automate data fetching from various sources, including APIs, databases, and web scraping.

8.3.1 Using APIs

Many platforms provide RESTful APIs that allow you to programmatically access their data. The `requests` library simplifies this process:

```python
import requests

response = requests.get('https://api.example.com/data')
data = response.json()
```

8.3.2 Web Scraping Tools

For data that isn't available via an API, web scraping can be an effective solution. Libraries such as `BeautifulSoup` and `Scrapy` are essential for extracting data from HTML pages.

```python
from bs4 import BeautifulSoup
import requests

url = 'https://example.com'
page = requests.get(url)

soup = BeautifulSoup(page.content, 'html.parser')

# Extract data (e.g., titles)
titles = soup.find_all('h1')
for title in titles:
    print(title.get_text())
```

8.4 Data Cleaning Automation

Data cleaning is a critical step in the analysis process, often consuming more time than analysis itself. Python offers tools to automate data cleaning routines.

8.4.1 Using Pandas for Data Cleaning

The `pandas` library provides DataFrame objects and operations that simplify the cleaning process. Common tasks include handling missing values, removing duplicates, and converting data types.

```python
import pandas as pd

# Load dataset
df = pd.read_csv('data.csv')

# Handle missing values df.fillna(method='ffill', inplace=True)

# Remove duplicates df.drop_duplicates(inplace=True)

# Convert a column to datetime df['date'] = pd.to_datetime(df['date'])
```

8.4.2 Custom Functions for Data Cleaning

You can create custom functions that encapsulate specific cleaning tasks. Automated scripts can then call these functions as needed.

```python
def clean_column(column):

column = column.str.lower().str.strip() return column

df['column_name'] = clean_column(df['column_name'])
```

8.5 Data Analysis Automation

Once the data is clean, the analytical process can begin. Python provides powerful libraries for statistical analysis, machine learning, and visualization.

8.5.1 Automation with Functions

Encapsulating frequently used analysis steps in functions can streamline your workflow.

```python
def summarize_data(df):

return df.describe()

summary = summarize_data(df)
```

8.5.2 Using Pipelines for Machine Learning

The `scikit-learn` library offers a pipeline mechanism that can streamline preprocessing and modeling steps:

```python
```

```
from sklearn.pipeline import Pipeline

from sklearn.preprocessing import StandardScaler from
sklearn.linear_model import LogisticRegression

pipeline = Pipeline([ ('scaler', StandardScaler()),

('model', LogisticRegression())

])

X = df[['feature1', 'feature2']] y = df['target']

pipeline.fit(X, y)
```
```

## 8.6 Automating Visualization

Visual representation of data is crucial for effective
communication. Python libraries such as `Matplotlib` and
`Seaborn` can be used to automate the creation of
visualizations.

### 8.6.1 Automation through Functions
```

You can create functions that generate specific types of plots based on input data:

```python
import seaborn as sns

import matplotlib.pyplot as plt

def plot_distribution(data, column):

sns.histplot(data[column],                    kde=True)
plt.title(f'Distribution of {column}') plt.show()

plot_distribution(df, 'column_name')
```

8.6.2 Reporting Automation

Utilizing libraries like `Matplotlib` and `ReportLab`, you can automate the generation of reports that include data visualizations, statistics, and insights.

8.7 Scheduling Automated Workflows

Once your automation scripts are developed, scheduling them to run at specific intervals can be accomplished using tools like `cron` (on UNIX systems) or Windows Task Scheduler.

8.7.1 Using Cron Jobs

To schedule a Python script to run daily at midnight, you might set up a cron job as follows:

```

0 0 * * * /usr/bin/python3 /path/to/your_script.py
```

By establishing a solid foundation in automation
128

principles, data experts can tackle complex datasets rapidly and reliably. Whether through API data fetching, web scraping, or automated visualization, Python's capabilities empower users to transform their data workflows into streamlined processes. As the volume of data grows, so too will the importance of automation in the field of data analysis.

Performing Statistical Analysis in Excel with Python

Excel has long been the go-to software for many analysts due to its user-friendly interface and powerful functionalities. However, when it comes to more advanced statistical analysis, Python provides an extensive array of libraries and tools that can enhance productivity and accuracy. This chapter explores the synergy of Excel and Python for statistical analysis, guiding you through the process of conducting such analyses effectively.

1. Introduction to Statistical Analysis

Statistical analysis involves the collection, examination, interpretation, and presentation of data in order to uncover patterns, test hypotheses, or make decisions based on data. It includes descriptive statistics—summarizing features of a dataset, inferential statistics—making predictions or inferences about a population based on a sample, and various other analyses like regression, ANOVA, and hypothesis testing.

2. Why Use Excel and Python Together?

While Excel is excellent for straightforward calculations and data visualization, Python excels at handling larger datasets, performing complex statistical computations, and automating repetitive tasks. Integrating both allows analysts to leverage the ease of Excel's interface while tapping into Python's analytical capabilities.

Advantages of Combining Excel with Python:

Ease of Use: Excel is accessible, making it easier for users without a programming background to interact with data.

Advanced Analytics: Python's libraries such as pandas, NumPy, and SciPy can perform sophisticated statistical operations that would be cumbersome in Excel.

Automation and Reproducibility: With Python, analysts can automate repetitive tasks and ensure that analyses are reproducible.

Enhanced Visualization: Python, with libraries like Matplotlib and Seaborn, offers more advanced data visualization options.

3. Setting Up Your Environment

To perform statistical analysis using Python in conjunction with Excel, follow these steps: ### 3.1 Requirements

Make sure that you have the following installed on your system:

Microsoft Excel: Version 2016 or later is recommended.

Python: Version 3.X.

Libraries: Install essential libraries using pip:

```bash
```

pip install pandas openpyxl numpy scipy matplotlib seaborn
```

### 3.2 Loading Data from Excel

You can load data from Excel into Python using the pandas library, which provides the `read_excel` function.

```python
import pandas as pd

# Load the Excel file

file_path = 'path_to_your_excel_file.xlsx'

data = pd.read_excel(file_path, sheet_name='Sheet1')

# Display the first few rows of the dataframe
print(data.head())
```

4. Conducting Descriptive Statistics

Once you have your data loaded, performing descriptive statistics is straightforward. Use the `describe()` method to obtain summary statistics.

```python
# Get descriptive statistics descriptive_stats = data.describe() print(descriptive_stats)
```

5. Performing Inferential Statistics ### 5.1 Hypothesis Testing

For hypothesis testing, you might want to perform a t-test to compare the means of two groups.
```

```python
from scipy import stats

# Assuming `GroupA` and `GroupB` are columns in your Excel file
group_a = data['GroupA'].dropna()

group_b = data['GroupB'].dropna()

# Conduct T-test

t_stat, p_val = stats.ttest_ind(group_a, group_b)
print(f"T-statistic: {t_stat}, P-value: {p_val}")
```

5.2 Regression Analysis

To carry out a regression analysis, you can use the `statsmodels` library, which allows you to fit linear models.

```python
import statsmodels.api as sm

# Assuming 'Y' is dependent and 'X' is independent variable
X = data['X']

Y = data['Y']

# Add a constant to the predictor variable
X = sm.add_constant(X)


# Fit regression model
model = sm.OLS(Y, X).fit()

# Display the regression results
print(model.summary())
```

6. Data Visualization

132

Visualizing statistical results can enhance understanding. Use Matplotlib or Seaborn to create visualizations. ### 6.1 Scatter Plot for Regression

```python
import matplotlib.pyplot as plt import seaborn as sns
```

Create a scatter plot plt.figure(figsize=(10, 6)) sns.regplot(x='X', y='Y', data=data) plt.title('Scatter Plot with Regression Line') plt.xlabel('X Variable')

plt.ylabel('Y Variable') plt.show()
```

## 7. Exporting Results Back to Excel

After completing your analysis, you might want to export results back to Excel.

```python
# Save the descriptive statistics to a new Excel file descriptive_stats.to_excel('descriptive_stats.xlsx', index=True)

# If you want to add results from the regression model (like coefficients) regression_results = pd.DataFrame(model.params, columns=['Coefficient']) regression_results.to_excel('regression_results.xlsx', index=True)
```

Combining Excel's accessibility with Python's powerful data analysis capabilities allows analysts to conduct comprehensive statistical analyses with ease. This integration not only enhances the efficiency of data workflows but also improves the accuracy and
```

reproducibility of statistical results. By following the methods outlined in this chapter, you can harness the best of both worlds, leading to more informed decision-making and deeper insights from your data.

Visualizing Data Using Python Libraries

Python, a powerful programming language, offers a variety of libraries that make it easy to create visual representations of data. In this chapter, we will explore some of the most popular Python libraries for data visualization, including Matplotlib, Seaborn, Plotly, and Altair, along with practical examples that demonstrate their capabilities.

1. The Importance of Data Visualization

Before diving into the libraries, it's important to understand why data visualization is crucial in the field of data science:

Clarity: Complex datasets can often be overwhelming. Visualizations help distill information into digestible visuals, making it easier to grasp insights.

Patterns and Trends: A well-designed visualization can reveal patterns and trends that may not be immediately obvious in raw data.

Storytelling: Data visualization is a critical tool for storytelling in data science. A compelling visualization communicates findings effectively to stakeholders.

2. Matplotlib: The Foundation of Data Visualization

Matplotlib is one of the oldest and most widely used libraries in Python for creating static visuals. It provides a flexible framework that allows users to create a range of plots including line charts, bar graphs, and scatter plots.

Example: Simple Line Plot

```python
import matplotlib.pyplot as plt import numpy as np

x = np.linspace(0, 10, 100) y = np.sin(x)

plt.figure(figsize=(10, 5))

plt.plot(x, y, label='Sine Wave', color='blue') plt.title('Sine Wave Example')

plt.xlabel('X-axis')        plt.ylabel('Y-axis')        plt.legend()
plt.grid(True) plt.show()
```

This example demonstrates how to create a simple line plot of a sine wave using Matplotlib. ## 3. Seaborn: A Higher-Level Interface

Seaborn builds on top of Matplotlib and provides a higher-level interface for drawing attractive and informative statistical graphics. It simplifies the process of creating complex visualizations and comes with several built-in themes to enhance the aesthetics.

Example: Pairplot of Iris Dataset

```python
import seaborn as sns import pandas as pd

# Load the Iris dataset

iris = sns.load_dataset('iris')

# Create a pairplot
```

135

```python
sns.pairplot(iris, hue='species', markers=['o', 's', 'D'])
plt.show()
```

Here, we use Seaborn to create a pairplot of the Iris dataset, which helps visualize relationships between different features, colored by species.

4. Plotly: Interactive Visualizations

Plotly allows for the creation of interactive visualizations, making it a powerful tool for web-based applications and dashboards. Users can hover over elements to see more information, zoom in, and filter data dynamically.

Example: Interactive Scatter Plot

```python
import plotly.express as px

# Load the Gapminder dataset gapminder = px.data.gapminder()
# Create an interactive scatter plot
fig = px.scatter(gapminder, x='gdpPercap', y='lifeExp', color='continent', size='pop', hover_name='country',

title='GDP per Capita vs Life Expectancy') fig.show()
```

In this example, we create an interactive scatter plot to visualize the relationship between GDP per capita and life expectancy across different countries.

5. Altair: Declarative Visualization

Altair is another declarative statistical visualization library for Python that offers a user-friendly API and a unique approach to creating visualizations based on the Vega-Lite grammar of graphics.

Example: Bar Chart with Altair

```python
import altair as alt
# Load the Titanic dataset
titanic = sns.load_dataset('titanic')
# Create a bar chart for passenger class distribution chart = alt.Chart(titanic).mark_bar().encode(
x='class', y='count()', color='sex',
tooltip=['class', 'count()']
).properties(
title='Titanic Passenger Class Distribution'
)
chart.show()
```

In this example, we use Altair to create an informative bar chart that visualizes the distribution of passengers across different classes, segmented by gender.

6. Choosing the Right Library

When selecting a library for data visualization, consider the following factors:

Complexity of Visualization: For simple static plots, Matplotlib or Seaborn might suffice, while more complex visualizations may benefit from Plotly or Altair.

Interactivity: If interactivity is a key requirement, Plotly is more suitable.

Aesthetics: Seaborn and Altair provide attractive default color palettes to enhance visual appeal.

Familiarity and Community Support: Matplotlib has extensive documentation and community support, making it a good starting point for beginners.

In this chapter, we explored the foundational libraries—Matplotlib and Seaborn—along with interactive options like Plotly and the declarative style used in Altair. By mastering these tools, you can effectively communicate your findings and tell compelling data stories. As you continue your journey in data visualization, keep experimenting with different libraries and techniques to enhance your skills and broaden your toolkit.

Chapter 9: Error Handling and Debugging Python Excel Scripts

In this chapter, we delve into the crucial aspects of error handling and debugging when working with Python scripts designed for Excel automation or data manipulation. As you enhance your skills in Python, you'll encounter various errors and bugs that could potentially derail your projects. Understanding how to identify, manage, and rectify these issues is vital for writing robust and efficient code.

Understanding Common Errors in Python

Before diving into error handling and debugging, it's essential to recognize the common types of errors you might face while scripting in Python:

Syntax Errors: These occur when Python encounters code that does not conform to proper syntax. They prevent your script from running and are generally easy to identify since Python will provide a specific error message pointing to the line where the mistake occurred.

Runtime Errors: These errors arise during the execution of the script, often due to invalid operations or nonexistent variables. Examples include division by zero or attempting to access an index that is out of range.

Logical Errors: These are arguably the most subtle and often the hardest to detect. The script runs without any syntax or runtime errors, but the output is not what you expect. This could be due to incorrect assumptions in your code or misunderstandings of the underlying data.

By familiarizing yourself with these types of errors, you

can better anticipate where things might go wrong and approach your debugging process with a clear framework.

Employing the Try-Except Block

One of the cornerstones of error handling in Python is the `try-except` block. This syntax allows you to "try" a block of code and "catch" exceptions as they arise, preventing the entire script from crashing.

Example:

```python
import pandas as pd

try:

df = pd.read_excel('data.xlsx') except FileNotFoundError:

print("Error: The file 'data.xlsx' was not found.")
```

In this example, if the specified Excel file is not found, rather than raising an unhandled exception that halts your script, it instead captures the error and prints a user-friendly message.

Catching Multiple Exceptions

You can also handle multiple exceptions elegantly with the `try-except` structure:

```python
try:
    df = pd.read_excel('data.xlsx')
    # Assume we are performing some data manipulation
    result = df['Column1'].mean()
except FileNotFoundError:
    print("Error: The file 'data.xlsx' was not found.")
except KeyError:
    print("Error: Column1 not found in the Excel file.")
```

In this case, if the file is missing, it will provide feedback about that. If the file is present but doesn't contain the specified column, it will handle that error too.

Finally Clause

You might also find the `finally` clause useful. Code within this block will execute regardless of whether an error occurred, making it ideal for cleanup actions.

```python
try:
    df = pd.read_excel('data.xlsx')
except Exception as e:
    print(f"An error occurred: {e}")
finally:
    print("Execution completed.")
```

Logging Errors for Review

One best practice in error handling is to log detailed error messages rather than simply printing them to the console. This is essential for troubleshooting more complex scripts, especially those that run in production.

141

To implement logging, Python's built-in `logging` module can be employed.

```python
import logging

logging.basicConfig(level=logging.ERROR, filename='error_log.txt') try:

df = pd.read_excel('data.xlsx')

except Exception as e:

logging.error("An error occurred: %s", str(e))
```

This logs errors to a file named `error_log.txt`, allowing you to review them later on. This is particularly advantageous when the script is part of a larger automated task.

Debugging Techniques

Debugging is the process of locating and fixing bugs in your code, and the following techniques can help you in this quest:

1. Print Statements

Simple yet effective, inserting print statements can help you track the flow of your program and the state of your variables at various points. However, this can become unwieldy in complex scripts.

2. Python Debugger (pdb)

For a more structured approach, consider using the built-in debugger, `pdb`. You can set breakpoints, step through your code line-by-line, and inspect variable values.

```python
import pdb

def process_data():

    df = pd.read_excel('data.xlsx')
    pdb.set_trace()  # Execution will pause here
    # Perform operations on df
```

This allows for a more interactive debugging experience.

3. Integrated Development Environment (IDE) Tools

Many IDEs, like PyCharm or Visual Studio Code, offer powerful debugging tools that allow you to set breakpoints, inspect variables, and execute code line by line. Familiarizing yourself with these features can significantly ease the debugging process.

As you continue your Python journey, remember that encountering and addressing errors is not just a part of programming; it is an important aspect that enhances your learning and understanding of the language.

Approach each error with curiosity, learn from it, and let it guide you to write better code in the future.

Common Errors and Their Solutions in Excel With Python

Understanding these common errors and how to address them is crucial for anyone looking to work efficiently and effectively with Excel in Python. This chapter will explore some of the most frequently encountered issues, along with their solutions.

1. File Not Found Error ### Overview

One of the most common errors encountered when working with Excel files in Python is the "File Not

Found" error. This occurs when the specified path to the Excel file is incorrect or the file does not exist in the given location.

Cause

The file path is incorrect.

The file has been moved or deleted.

Typographical errors in the file name or extension.

Solution

To resolve a "File Not Found" error, start by checking the file path and ensuring it is correctly specified. You can use the `os.path` module to verify the path:

```python
import os

file_path = 'path/to/excel_file.xlsx'
if not os.path.exists(file_path):
    print("File not found. Please check the path.")
```

Additionally, ensure that the file name, extension, and case sensitivity match exactly, especially on Unix-like systems.

2. Unsupported File Format Error ### Overview

When attempting to read an Excel file using libraries like `pandas` or `openpyxl`, you might encounter an

"Unsupported File Format" error.

Cause

This generally occurs when the file being accessed is not in the correct format (e.g., attempting to read a

`.csv` or `.txt` file with the `read_excel` function) or is corrupt.

Solution

Make sure you are using the correct file extension and format. If you are dealing with a `.csv` file, for example, use:

```python
import pandas as pd

df = pd.read_csv('file.csv')
```

If the file is indeed an Excel file but still shows this error, consider re-saving the file using Excel or another spreadsheet tool, as this may correct any issues with the file format.

3. ValueError: Length of Values Mismatch ### Overview

A "ValueError" can occur when trying to assign a list or array of values to a DataFrame column if the length

of the values does not match the number of rows in the DataFrame.

Cause

The number of values you are trying to insert does not match the existing number of rows in the DataFrame.

Solution

Make sure that the length of the list or array matches the DataFrame's length. You can check the shape of your DataFrame and the length of your values:

```python
import pandas as pd
# Example DataFrame data = {'A': [1, 2, 3]}
df = pd.DataFrame(data)
# Correcting the ValueError
new_values = [4, 5] # This will raise an error. if len(new_values) == len(df):
df['B'] = new_values else:
print("Length of new values does not match DataFrame length.")
```

4. ImportError: Missing Required Libraries ### Overview

If you attempt to run a function that requires a specific library (e.g., `openpyxl`, `xlsxwriter`), and that library is not installed, you may see an "ImportError."

Cause

The library needed for specific functionalities is not installed in your Python environment.

Solution

Ensure that all the required libraries are installed. You can do this using `pip`:

```bash
pip install openpyxl pandas xlsxwriter
```

After installing the required libraries, try running your code again. ## 5. SettingWithCopyWarning

Overview

When modifying a slice of a DataFrame, `pandas` may raise a `SettingWithCopyWarning`. This warning indicates that the operation may not do what you expect.

Cause

This warning happens when attempting to set values on a view of a DataFrame rather than on the DataFrame itself.

Solution

To avoid this warning, explicitly use the `.loc` indexer to ensure you are modifying the original DataFrame:

```python
import pandas as pd
df = pd.DataFrame({'A': [1, 2, 3], 'B': [4, 5, 6]})
```

```
# Correct way to set values df.loc[df['A'] == 2, 'B'] = 10
```

By using `.loc`, you ensure that you are explicitly referring to the original DataFrame. ## 6. MemoryError

Overview

If you are working with large Excel files, you might encounter a "MemoryError" due to insufficient memory to load the entire file into a DataFrame.

Cause

The DataFrame exceeds the memory limit of your system.

Solution

To handle large files efficiently, consider reading the Excel file in chunks or using parameters to read only necessary columns:

```python
import pandas as pd

# Read only specific columns

df = pd.read_excel('large_file.xlsx', usecols='A,C,F')

# Or read in chunks chunk_size = 10000

for chunk in pd.read_excel('large_file.xlsx', chunksize=chunk_size):

# Process each chunk process(chunk)
```

Working with Excel files in Python can lead to various errors, but understanding these common mistakes can significantly improve your debugging skills and efficiency.

By knowing how to troubleshoot file paths, format issues, DataFrame manipulations, and memory management, you can enhance your productivity when using Python for Excel data analysis and manipulation.

Debugging Techniques and Best Practices in Excel with Python

In the context of using Python to manipulate Excel files, an additional layer of challenge arises due to the intricate formatting, formulas, and connections inherent in spreadsheets. Effective debugging techniques can save developers time, avoid frustration, and ultimately lead to cleaner, more efficient code. This chapter will delve into various debugging techniques and best practices specifically aimed at Python developers working with Excel files, using libraries such as `pandas`, `openpyxl`, and `xlrd`.

Understanding the Environment ### Familiarity with Libraries

Before diving into debugging techniques, it's crucial to have a solid understanding of the libraries you'll be working with. Popular libraries like `pandas` for data manipulation, `openpyxl` for reading and writing Excel 2010 files, and `xlrd` for older Excel files are pivotal in managing Excel data through Python. Ensuring clarity on how to use these libraries will help you pinpoint where errors may occur during data handling.

Setting Up a Development Environment

Setting up a proper development environment can significantly impact your debugging process. Consider using:

Jupyter Notebooks: Ideal for data analysis and Excel manipulation, as they allow for immediate feedback and visualization.

Integrated Development Environments (IDEs): Tools like PyCharm, VSCode, or Spyder facilitate debugging with robust features, such as breakpoints, variable tracking, and real-time error detection.

Common Errors in Excel Manipulation with Python

Understanding common errors can frame your approach to debugging. Some common issues include:

File Not Found Errors: Ensure the file path is correct and that the file exists.

Data Type Mismatches: Excel contains strings, dates, and numbers; ensure you are handling each type correctly.

Formula Errors: If you're manipulating formulas directly in Excel, they may not work correctly when read or modified via Python.

Debugging Techniques ### 1. Print Statements

The simplest and most effective debugging technique is the use of `print` statements. Placing `print()` functions throughout your code helps you to track variable values and flow execution. For example:

```python
import pandas as pd

# Load the Excel file try:

data = pd.read_excel('data.xlsx') print("Data loaded
```

successfully.")

except Exception as e:

print(f"Error loading data: {e}")

Check data types print(data.dtypes)

` ` `

2. Exception Handling

Using `try-except` blocks can manage errors gracefully and allow for cleaner error reporting. This technique is particularly useful for reading files or manipulating data:

` ` `python try:

data = pd.read_excel('data.xlsx') except FileNotFoundError:

print("The specified file does not exist.") except ValueError as e:

print(f"Value error: {e}")

` ` `

3. Interactive Debuggers

Leveraging the built-in debugger in IDEs can allow you to pause execution, inspect variables, and step through code line by line. Using the `pdb` module can also help:

` ` `python import pdb

Setting a trace pdb.set_trace()

` ` `

This will drop you into an interactive environment where you can execute commands to inspect the state of your program.

151

4. Logging

Instead of print statements, for larger projects, consider using Python's `logging` module for a more robust solution. Logging provides different severity levels and is configurable, allowing you to control what messages are displayed.

```python
import logging

logging.basicConfig(level=logging.DEBUG)

logging.debug("This is a debug message")
logging.info("Loading Excel file.")
```

5. Assertions

Using assertions helps ensure that conditions you expect to be true at a certain point in your program hold. This can catch potential issues early on:

```python
assert not data.empty, "Dataframe is empty."
```

6. Unit Testing

Writing unit tests for your data manipulation functions can help catch bugs before they affect other parts of your code base. Libraries such as `unittest` or `pytest` can be employed to systematically verify that your functions operate as intended.

```python
import unittest

class TestExcelOperations(unittest.TestCase):
```

```python
def test_load_data(self):
    data                    = pd.read_excel('data.xlsx')
    self.assertEqual(data.shape[1], expected_columns)

if __name__ == '__main__':
    unittest.main()
```
```

## Best Practices

### 1. Write Clean, Readable Code

Adhere to PEP 8 standards for Python code style. Use meaningful variable names and proper documentation. Clean code reduces mistakes and aids in easier debugging.

### 2. Keep Excel Files Organized

Maintain a structured approach to your Excel files. Use consistent naming conventions, and keep track of your data formats and any required Excel-specific settings.

### 3. Validate Data at Every Step

Rather than waiting until the end of your data processing to discover issues, validate your data after each manipulation step. This involves checking for empty cells, valid types, and expected ranges.

### 4. Version Control

Make use of version control systems, such as Git, to track changes in your scripts and data files. Being able to revert changes quickly can be invaluable during the debugging process.

### 5. Continuous Learning
```

Stay updated with best practices and new tools in the Python ecosystem that can improve debugging processes. Online communities, documentation, and relevant literature can prove to be excellent resources.

With the right tools and mindset, addressing issues in your code becomes a less daunting task, paving the way for more efficient data analysis and manipulation tasks. Embrace these methods, and soon you'll confront bugs with confidence, ensuring smooth and seamless interactions with Excel through Python.

Chapter 10: Enhancing Excel Macros with Python Automation

However, there are limitations to what can be achieved using Excel's built-in Visual Basic for Applications (VBA). This chapter will explore the powerful synergy that can be achieved by integrating Python automation with Excel macros. Harnessing Python's capabilities allows users to extend functionality, improve performance, and simplify complex operations.

1. Understanding Excel Macros

Before diving into Python automation, it is essential to grasp the fundamentals of Excel macros. Macros are a series of commands that automate repetitive tasks. They can be recorded using Excel's built-in Macro Recorder or written using VBA. While they are helpful for straightforward tasks, they can become cumbersome for more complicated operations involving extensive data manipulation.

1.1 Creating a Simple Macro

To illustrate, let's create a simple macro that formats a selected range of cells. By following these steps, you might record a macro for formatting data to a consistent style, which can then be expanded upon with Python.

Open Excel and navigate to the "Developer" tab.

Click on "Record Macro" and give the macro a name (e.g., `FormatCells`).

Select the cells you want to format.

Use the formatting toolbar to adjust the font size, color,

and cell borders.

Stop recording the macro.

You can now run this macro anytime you need to format your data similarly. ## 2. The Limitations of VBA

While VBA is reasonably powerful for various tasks, it exhibits some limitations:

Performance: VBA may not handle large datasets efficiently as compared to Python, especially when dealing with advanced data analytics or machine learning.

Complex Data Manipulation: Advanced data science and analytics require libraries that VBA lacks, making Python a better choice.

Accessibility: Python is open-source and platform-independent, which allows greater collaboration and integration with other applications compared to VBA.

3. Python: A Better Alternative

Python has become a popular choice for data analysis and automation, thanks to its extensive libraries like

`pandas`, `openpyxl`, and `xlwings`. These libraries make it easy to read, manipulate, and write data in Excel files, enabling us to augment the capabilities of Excel macros significantly.

3.1 Setting Up Python for Excel Automation

To get started with Python automation for Excel, you'll need to set up your environment:

Install Python: Download and install Python from the official website (www.python.org).

Install Required Libraries:

Use pip to install essential libraries. Open your command prompt or terminal and run:

```bash
pip install pandas openpyxl xlwings
```

Configure Excel for Python Script Execution: For `xlwings`, ensure you enable the xlwings Excel add-in.

4. Integrating Python with Excel Macros ### 4.1 From VBA to Python

An example of migrating a simple macro to Python might take the following format. Imagine your VBA code looks like this for formatting:

```vba
Sub FormatCells() With Selection
.Font.Size = 12
.Font.Color = RGB(0, 0, 255)
.Borders.LineStyle = xlContinuous End With
End Sub
```

The equivalent Python code using `xlwings` would be:

```python
import xlwings as xw
def format_cells():
```

```python
wb = xw.Book.caller() sheet=wb.sheets.active
rng = sheet.range('A1:H10')  # Adjust the range as necessary


rng.font.size = 12
rng.font.color = (0, 0, 255) rng.api.Borders.LineStyle = 1 # xlContinuous
```

By calling this function from an Excel macro, you gain improved performance, and leveraging Python opens the door for more intricate algorithms and data processing.

4.2 Processing Large Datasets

One of the notable advantages of Python is its capacity to handle large datasets effortlessly. Let's say you want to analyze sales data; using `pandas`, you can easily load a CSV file, analyze it, and output the results back to Excel:

```python
import pandas as pd import xlwings as xw


def analyze_sales_data(file_path):
df = pd.read_csv(file_path)
summary   =   df.groupby('Product').agg({'Sales': 'sum'}).reset_index()


wb = xw.Book.caller()
sheet = wb.sheets['Summary'] sheet.range('A1').value =
```

summary
```

In this example, we first read the data using `pandas`, perform a group-by operation, and write the summary back to an Excel worksheet, all while requiring minimal modification of the existing macro structure.

## 5. Automating Workflow with Python and Excel

By automating your workflow with Python scripts, users can significantly enhance productivity. You can create scheduled tasks where Python scripts run based on triggers from your workflows in Excel, allowing for near-real-time data analysis and reporting.

### 5.1 Practical Use Cases: Reporting and Dashboards

Consider a scenario in a corporate environment where regular financial reporting is necessary. Using Python, you can automate the entire process, fetching data from APIs, processing it with machine learning models, and updating Excel with the results to present in a dashboard format.

```python
import requests
```

def update_financial_dashboard():

Fetch data from an API

response   =
requests.get('https://api.example.com/financials') data =
response.json()

df = pd.DataFrame(data) wb = xw.Book.caller()

sheet = wb.sheets['Financial Dashboard']
```

```
sheet.range('A1').value = df
```
```
```

Enhancing Excel macros with Python automation can drastically change your approach to data analysis and reporting. With Python's extensive libraries and capabilities, you can process and visualize data like never before. Users will not only save time but also empower their analytic abilities to make informed, data-driven decisions. As we move forward, integrating VBA with Python will become an essential skill for professionals looking to optimize their data workflows.

Scheduling and Automating Tasks in Excel With Python

Fortunately, Python, a versatile programming language, offers powerful tools to automate and schedule these tasks, enabling you to work more efficiently. This chapter will guide you through the process of scheduling and automating tasks in Excel using Python.

1. Introduction to Automation in Excel with Python

Automation in Excel can save significant time and reduce human error. By leveraging Python, you can write scripts that interact with Excel files, eliminating the need for manual intervention. Using libraries like

`pandas` and `openpyxl`, you can read, manipulate, and write Excel files seamlessly. Additionally, with tools like `schedule` and `pywin32`, you can run these scripts automatically at specified intervals or times.

1.1 Key Libraries for Automation

pandas: A powerful library primarily used for data

manipulation and analysis. It provides easy-to-use data structures like DataFrames, which can easily interface with Excel files.

openpyxl: A library to read and write Excel 2010 xlsx/xlsm/xltx/xltm files. It allows you to create new files, modify existing ones, and read data without needing Excel installed.

xlwings: A library that makes it easy to call Python from Excel and manipulate Excel from Python. It provides a seamless bridge between VBA and Python.

schedule: A lightweight library for scheduling tasks in Python, allowing you to run Python functions at regular intervals.

pywin32: A set of Python extensions for Windows that allows you to access Windows APIs, including automation of Excel through the COM interface.

2. Setting Up Your Environment

To begin automating Excel with Python, you need to set up your development environment. Follow these steps to install the required libraries.

2.1 Installing Python Libraries

You can install the necessary libraries using `pip`. Open your command line or terminal and run the following commands:

```bash

pip install pandas openpyxl schedule pywin32
```

2.2 Setting Up Excel

Ensure that you have Excel installed on your computer, especially if you plan to use `pywin32` for automation. Familiarize yourself with the structure of your Excel files and the sort of tasks you wish to automate.

3. Basic Automation Techniques

Once the libraries are installed, you can start automating tasks in Excel. Here are a few common tasks you can automate using Python.

3.1 Reading Excel Files

Using `pandas`, you can read data from an Excel file as follows:

```python
import pandas as pd

# Read an Excel file

df = pd.read_excel('data.xlsx', sheet_name='Sheet1')
print(df.head())
```

3.2 Writing to Excel Files

Once you've processed your data, you can write the results back to an Excel file:

```python

# Suppose you manipulate your data here df['New Column'] = df['Existing Column'] * 2

# Write to a new Excel file df.to_excel('output.xlsx', index=False)
```

163

```
```

3.3 Modifying Existing Excel Files

To modify existing Excel files, you can use `openpyxl`:

```python
from openpyxl import load_workbook

# Load an existing workbook

wb = load_workbook('existing_file.xlsx') ws = wb.active

# Modify a cell value ws['A1'] = 'Updated Value'

# Save the workbook wb.save('existing_file.xlsx')
```

4. Scheduling Tasks with Python

Once you have your automation scripts ready, you can schedule them to run at specified times using the `schedule` library.

4.1 Scheduling a Task

Here's a simple example of how to schedule a task that runs a function every day at a specified time:

```python
import schedule import time
def job():
    print("Running scheduled job...")
    # Call your function here (e.g., data processing)

    # Schedule the job
```

```
schedule.every().day.at("10:00").do(job)

while True:

schedule.run_pending() time.sleep(1)
```
```

You can place your data processing function inside the `job` function, allowing it to run automatically at the scheduled time.

## 5. Advanced Scheduling with Windows Task Scheduler

If you wish to run your Python script at a more sophisticated level, you can use Windows Task Scheduler. This allows your script to run at startup, logon, or at specific intervals. Here's a brief overview:

### 5.1 Creating a Task in Windows Task Scheduler

Open **Task Scheduler** from the start menu.

Click on **Create Basic Task** in the Actions pane.

Follow the wizard to set the name, description, trigger, and action (select to run your Python executable with the path to your script as an argument).

Configure any additional settings and save the task.

This method ensures that your task runs even when you're not actively using Python or Excel.

In this chapter, we explored the fundamentals of scheduling and automating tasks in Excel using Python. By leveraging libraries such as `pandas`, `openpyxl`, and `schedule`, you can streamline your workflow, reduce the potential for errors, and reclaim your time.

The ability to automate tedious tasks not only enhances
```

productivity but also provides room for more strategic thinking and data analysis. With your new knowledge, you're well on your way to mastering Excel automation with Python—a skill that is becoming increasingly valuable in today's data-driven world.

Creating Python-Driven Excel Dashboards

Dashboards serve as a powerful means of visualizing data, allowing users to see trends, patterns, and key performance indicators at a glance. Excel has long been a favored tool for business intelligence, providing a platform rich with functionalities for data manipulation and visualization. However, when combined with Python, the capabilities of Excel for creating dynamic and interactive dashboards are significantly enhanced. This chapter will guide you through the process of leveraging Python to create robust dashboards in Excel, allowing for automation, advanced data analysis, and an improved user experience.

1. Understanding the Basics

Before we dive into building our dashboard, it is crucial to have a solid understanding of the tools we will use:

1.1 Python: The Powerhouse

Python is a versatile programming language known for its simplicity and readability. With libraries such as Pandas, Matplotlib, and Seaborn, Python allows you to manipulate data, analyze it, and create visualizations with ease. Python's capability to handle large datasets and perform complex calculations can significantly enhance the functionality of your Excel dashboards.

1.2 Excel: The Palpable Interface

Excel remains a widely used application for data analysis and visualization. It offers numerous built-in functions, chart types, and data manipulation tools that make it user-friendly. With Python, we can automate repetitive tasks, enrich data analysis, and generate visual content that enhances Excel's native functionality.

1.3 Integrating Python with Excel

Python and Excel can be integrated through various libraries, such as `openpyxl`, `xlsxwriter`, and `pandas`. These libraries allow Python to create, modify, and manipulate Excel files programmatically.

2. Preparing Your Environment

To create Python-driven Excel dashboards, you'll need to set up your environment. Here's how to do that: ### 2.1 Installing Python

Ensure you have Python installed on your machine. You can download it from the official Python website (https://www.python.org/).

2.2 Setting Up Libraries

Use pip to install the necessary libraries. In your command line or terminal, execute the following:

```bash
pip install pandas openpyxl xlsxwriter matplotlib seaborn
```

These libraries will help with data manipulation, Excel file handling, and creating visualizations. ### 2.3 Choosing an IDE

Select a suitable Integrated Development Environment

(IDE) for Python. Jupyter Notebook and Visual Studio Code are popular choices as they provide a user-friendly interface for coding and testing your scripts.

3. Building Your Data Pipeline ### 3.1 Importing and Cleaning Data

Begin by importing your data into Python using Pandas. The following example demonstrates how to load data from a CSV file:

```python
import pandas as pd

# Load data

data = pd.read_csv('your_data_file.csv')

# Display the first few rows print(data.head())
```

Clean and preprocess your data as needed. Common cleaning steps include:

Handling missing values

Renaming columns for clarity

Filtering data to focus on key metrics

```python
# Handling missing values data.fillna(method='ffill', inplace=True)

# Renaming columns

data.rename(columns={'OldName':     'NewName'}, inplace=True)
```

3.2 Analyzing Data

Once the data is clean, perform any necessary analysis to derive insights. This can include:

Grouping data for summarization

Calculating aggregations (e.g., sum, average)

```python
# Grouping data

summary = data.groupby('Category').sum()

# Calculate averages average_values = data.mean()
```

4. Creating Visualizations

Visualizations are crucial for any dashboard. You can either create them directly in Python or as embedded charts in Excel.

4.1 Using Matplotlib and Seaborn

For more intricate visualizations, create plots using Matplotlib and Seaborn. Here's a simple example of creating a bar chart:

```python
import matplotlib.pyplot as plt import seaborn as sns

# Creating a bar plot

sns.barplot(x='Category', y='Value', data=summary.reset_index()) plt.title('Category Summary') plt.savefig('category_summary.png') # Save the visualization plt.show()
```

4.2 Embedding Visualizations in Excel

Now, let's embed the visualization within an Excel file. The `xlsxwriter` library allows us to add images to our workbook:

```python
import xlsxwriter

# Creating a new Excel file

workbook = xlsxwriter.Workbook('Dashboard.xlsx') worksheet = workbook.add_worksheet()

# Insert the image

worksheet.insert_image('A1', 'category_summary.png')

# Close the workbook workbook.close()
```

5. Creating Interactive Dashboards

Excel has interactive features like drop-down menus,

slicers, and pivot tables, which can be enhanced with Python-generated data. Here's a simple implementation with sample controls.

5.1 Dynamic Data through Parameterization

By adjusting data dynamically using parameters in your Python script, you can create a more interactive dashboard:

```python
def update_dashboard(filter_value):

filtered_data = data[data['Category'] == filter_value] # Any analysis based on the filtered data

return filtered_data

```

5.2 Refreshing Data

To keep your dashboard up-to-date, consider implementing a script that fetches data at defined intervals or upon specific triggers.

6. Final Touches and Automation ### 6.1 Adding Formatting and Styles

Utilize `xlsxwriter` for advanced formatting when writing to an Excel workbook. This can improve the aesthetic and usability of your dashboard.

6.2 Scheduling Tasks

To fully automate the dashboard creation, schedule your Python script using Task Scheduler (Windows) or cron jobs (Unix-based systems). This allows for periodic updates without manual intervention.

In this chapter, we explored how to create Python-driven Excel dashboards by integrating Python's data handling capabilities with Excel's visualization strengths. Leveraging libraries such as Pandas, Matplotlib, and XlsxWriter, we demonstrated how to create a powerful tool that can enhance data comprehension and decision-making.

Chapter 11: Converting Existing VBA Macros to Python Efficiently

This chapter aims to guide readers through the process of converting existing VBA macros to Python efficiently, covering the rationale for the conversion, the tools required, and strategies for a successful transition.

Understanding the Need for Conversion

1. General Advantages of Python Over VBA

The decision to convert VBA macros to Python is driven by several overarching benefits:

Cross-Platform Compatibility: Python runs on various operating systems, whereas VBA is confined to Windows environments with Microsoft Office. This makes Python a more versatile choice for wider deployment.

Rich Ecosystem and Libraries: Python boasts a wealth of libraries such as Pandas, NumPy, and openpyxl, which provide robust functionalities for data manipulation and analysis that extend far beyond what VBA can offer.

Improved Performance and Scalability: Python can handle larger datasets more efficiently and can be integrated with databases, APIs, and web services, thereby optimizing data workflows.

Modern Syntax and Ease of Use: Python's clean and readable syntax often leads to faster development and easier debugging, making it accessible for beginners and experts alike.

2. Assessing Existing VBA Code

Before jumping into the conversion, it's crucial to conduct

a thorough assessment of the existing VBA macros. This involves:

Identifying frequently-used functions and routines within the macros that need to be retained in Python.

Evaluating the complexity of the code, noting any advanced features like user forms, error handling, or custom builds.

Documenting the current workflow to establish a clear understanding of how users interact with the macros.

Tools for Conversion

1. Python Libraries for Excel Manipulation

Adapting VBA macros to Python requires a toolset that can interact efficiently with Excel files. Here are some libraries you should consider:

openpyxl: This library allows for reading and writing Excel 2010 xlsx/xlsm/xltx/xltm files, enabling users to manipulate worksheets and create dynamic reports.

Pandas: While it's primarily a data manipulation library, Pandas integrates seamlessly with Excel through functions like `read_excel()` and `to_excel()`, making it perfect for data analysis.

xlrd and xlwt: These libraries are used for reading and writing older Excel formats (xls). While their usage has declined in favor of openpyxl and Pandas, they can still play a role in specific legacy projects.

2. IDEs and Development Tools

Choose appropriate development environments for writing and testing your Python scripts:

Jupyter Notebooks: Ideal for iterative development, Jupyter provides an interactive interface for testing small code snippets, making it easier to visualize data and results.

PyCharm or Visual Studio Code: Both are powerful IDEs that provide comprehensive support for Python development, including debugging, testing, and Git integration.

Guidelines for Conversion

1. Breaking Down the Macro Logic

Divide the existing VBA macro into logical segments. Focus on taking one modular component at a time and translating it, ensuring that the functionality remains intact through the conversion.

Identify Functionality: List all of the specific tasks your VBA code executes. For example, does it retrieve data, manipulate it, or create charts? Categorizing functionality will help target equivalent libraries in Python.

Stub Out Functions: Create Python functions that mirror the structure of VBA subroutines. Start with stubs that outline input parameters and expected outputs.

2. Writing Equivalent Python Code

With a clear breakdown of the functionality, begin converting the VBA code to Python. Here are some common translations to consider:

Variable Declaration: In VBA, variables are explicitly declared with types—`Dim x As Integer`—while Python uses dynamic typing: `x = 0`.

Control Structures: VBA uses constructs such as `For...Next`, `If...Then`, and `Select Case`, which translate to Python's `for`, `if`, and `switch` respectively in a more streamlined syntax.

Error Handling: VBA uses `On Error GoTo`, whereas Python employs `try...except` blocks, offering more robust and flexible error management.

3. Testing and Validation

After coding, it's essential to rigorously test the Python implementation against the original VBA macros. Ensure that the following steps are fulfilled:

Validation Checks: Cross-reference outputs of the Python script with those generated by the original VBA macro to identify discrepancies.

Unit Testing: Use libraries like `unittest` or `pytest` to automate the testing process, ensuring that each function performs as expected under various scenarios.

User Acceptance Testing (UAT): Involve stakeholders in the testing phase to confirm that the new Python-based solution meets their needs and replicated VBA behavior.

Performance Optimization

Once your Python implementation is functioning correctly, look into potential performance enhancements. Some strategies include:

Vectorization: Use vectorized operations available in libraries like NumPy and Pandas to operate on entire arrays of data rather than iterating through them with loops.

Parallel Processing: For extremely large datasets or computationally intensive tasks, consider leveraging libraries like `multiprocessing` to distribute work across multiple CPU cores.

Profile Your Code: Use profiling tools such as `cProfile` to identify bottlenecks in your script and optimize those specific areas for better performance.

The conversion of existing VBA macros to Python is a significant step towards modernizing data manipulation and analysis workflows. By understanding the advantages of Python, assessing the existing VBA code, leveraging appropriate tools and libraries, and adhering to best practices in programming and testing, developers can ensure a smooth transition. As we move forward into a data-driven future, adapting to new technologies not only enhances productivity but also equips organizations with the agility needed to thrive.

Analyzing and Mapping VBA Code to Python

Visual Basic for Applications (VBA) has long been a staple in environments like Microsoft Excel, providing users with a robust tool for automating tasks, manipulating datasets, and creating custom functions.

However, as the programming landscape evolves, many developers and data analysts are turning to Python due to its versatility, ease of learning, and a vast ecosystem of libraries. This chapter delves into the process of analyzing and mapping VBA code to Python, empowering readers to transition smoothly from VBA programming to Python development while maintaining their productivity.

Understanding the Basics

Overview of VBA and Python

Before we embark on the journey of mapping VBA to Python, it is crucial to understand the fundamental differences between the two languages:

VBA is primarily used for automating tasks within Microsoft Office applications. It features a relatively straightforward syntax, making it accessible to non-developers.

Python, on the other hand, is a general-purpose programming language known for its readability and extensive libraries for data manipulation, web development, machine learning, and more.

With this foundational knowledge, we can now move forward with the analysis and transformation process. ## Analyzing VBA Code

Structure of VBA

To effectively analyze and convert VBA code, one must first understand its components:

Subroutines: Defined by the `Sub` keyword, these are blocks of code that perform specific tasks.

Functions: Similar to subroutines but return a value,

defined using the `Function` keyword.

Variables and Data Types: VBA has a variety of built-in data types (e.g., Integer, String, Boolean) and allows for user-defined types.

Example of VBA Code

```vba
Sub CalculateSum() Dim total As Integer Dim i As Integer

total = 0
For i = 1 To 10 total = total + i
Next i


MsgBox "The total is " & total End Sub
```

Key Components to Analyze

Control Structures: Loops, conditionals (`If...Then`, `For`, `Do While`), and error handling (`On Error`) must be identified as they will be translated into Python syntax.

Data Structures: Understand the use of arrays, collections (`Collection`, `Dictionary`), and how data is stored and manipulated.

Excel Objects: Recognize interactions with the Excel application, such as accessing worksheets, ranges, and cells.

Mapping VBA to Python

Once the VBA code is analyzed, we can begin the mapping process. ### Syntax Conversion

The first step in translating VBA code to Python is converting the syntax. Python uses a different syntax for defining functions, control structures, and variables.

Example Mapping

VBA Code:

```vba
If total > 0 Then

MsgBox "Total is positive" Else

MsgBox "Total is not positive" End If
```

Equivalent Python Code:

```python
if total > 0:
print("Total is positive") else:
print("Total is not positive")
```

Libraries and Functions

Python leverages built-in functions and libraries to replicate functionalities available in VBA:

NumPy/Pandas: For numerical operations and data manipulation.

Tkinter or PyQt: For creating graphical user interfaces (similar to message boxes in VBA).

OpenPyXL or xlwings: To interact with Excel files.

Example of Data Manipulation

VBA Code:

```vba
Range("A1").Value = total
```

Equivalent Python Code using OpenPyXL:

```python
from openpyxl import Workbook
wb = Workbook() ws = wb.active ws['A1'] = total
wb.save('output.xlsx')
```

Error Handling

VBA employs the `On Error` statement for error handling, whereas Python uses `try...except` blocks.

VBA Code:

```vba
On Error GoTo ErrorHandler  ' Code that may cause an error Exit Sub
ErrorHandler:
MsgBox "An error occurred!"
```

Equivalent Python Code:

```python try:
# Code that may cause an error except Exception as e:
```

```
print("An error occurred:", e)
```
```

```

Testing and Validation

After mapping the code, thorough testing and validation are critical to ensure that the Python version of the code functions as expected. This involves:

Unit Testing: Creating test cases to validate individual functions or modules.

Integration Testing: Testing the interaction between different parts of the system.

Performance Testing: Ensuring that the Python code executes efficiently, especially when handling large datasets.

. By systematically analyzing VBA code and mapping it to Python, developers can harness the full power of both languages, leveraging the strengths of each. This chapter provides a framework to facilitate this transformation, enabling readers to effectively navigate their coding journey from VBA to Python. As we continue in this book, we will explore more specific libraries, techniques, and best practices for Python programming in data-centric environments.

Techniques for Seamless Conversion VBA Macros to Python

Visual Basic for Applications (VBA) has long been a staple in the world of Microsoft Office automation. However, with the rise of Python, a language renowned for its simplicity and an expansive ecosystem of libraries, many users are eager to make the switch. This chapter explores the process of converting VBA macros to Python scripts, highlighting the similarities and differences, and providing detailed guidance for transitioning your automation tasks seamlessly.

Why Transition from VBA to Python?

Versatility: Python's applications go far beyond what is possible with VBA. From data analysis with libraries like Pandas and NumPy to web development with frameworks like Flask and Django, Python offers a framework for virtually any type of programming task.

Community Support: Python has a vast community and a wealth of resources that facilitate problem- solving and learning, making it easier to find help and libraries suitable for almost any use case.

Cross-Platform Compatibility: Unlike VBA, which is tied to Microsoft Office, Python is a cross- platform language that can run on numerous operating systems, making it more adaptable in diverse environments.

Modern Development Practices: Python naturally supports modern programming paradigms, such as object-oriented programming and functional programming, which can lead to cleaner and more maintainable code than what is often achieved through VBA.

Understanding VBA

Before diving into the transition process, it's essential to understand the core components of a VBA macro. A typical VBA macro consists of:

Subroutines: Blocks of code that perform specific operations.

Variables: Objects or data types that store information for processing.

Control Structures: If statements, loops (For, While), and error handling mechanisms that enable more complex logic.

Excel Objects: References to workbooks, worksheets, ranges, and charts, which are heavily utilized in office automation tasks.

Example VBA Macro

Let's consider a simple example of a VBA macro that loops through all cells in a selected range and highlights cells that contain values greater than 100.

```vba
Sub HighlightCells() Dim cell As Range

For Each cell In Selection If cell.Value > 100 Then

cell.Interior.Color = RGB(255, 0, 0) ' Highlight in red End If

Next cell End Sub
```

Translating VBA to Python

Setting Up Python Environment

Before translating the code, you'll need a proper Python environment set up. This typically includes installing an IDE (like PyCharm or Visual Studio Code) and necessary libraries, such as `pandas` for data manipulation and `openpyxl` or `xlsxwriter` for Excel file handling.

```bash
pip install pandas openpyxl xlsxwriter
```

Example Conversion: Highlighting Cells

Now, let's translate the VBA macro we showcased earlier into Python. Below is how you can achieve similar functionality using Python.

```python
import pandas as pd
```

Load an Excel workbook and select a sheet file_path = 'path_to_your_excel_file.xlsx'

df = pd.read_excel(file_path, sheet_name='Sheet1')

Loop through the DataFrame and apply highlighting logic def highlight_cells(df):

def highlight(value): if value > 100:

return 'background-color: red' return ''

return df.style.applymap(highlight) styled_df = highlight_cells(df)

Save the styled DataFrame to a new Excel file styled_df.to_excel('highlighted_cells.xlsx', engine='openpyxl')
```
```

Key Differences

186

Syntax and Structure: Python uses indentation to signify code blocks, whereas VBA uses `Sub` and `End Sub` to define them.

Data Structures: VBA operates with arrays and ranges as its primary means for data storage, while Python utilizes data frames from libraries like Pandas, providing more powerful data manipulation capabilities.

Libraries: In Python, functionality is modularized through the use of libraries, whereas VBA offers a more monolithic approach tied to the Microsoft Office suite.

Benefits of the Python Approach

Readability: Python code is often more readable and simpler to understand due to its clear syntax.

Advanced Features: With libraries such as Pandas and NumPy, Python facilitates advanced data analysis techniques that are cumbersome in VBA.

Reusable Functions: Python allows the creation of functions that can be easily reused across different scripts.

Transitioning from VBA macros to Python scripts opens up a world of possibilities for data manipulation and automation. This chapter provided a basic framework for converting simple VBA scripts into Python, illustrating key similarities and differences. As you grow more comfortable with Python, you may discover new methods to enhance your workflows and empower your data analysis processes. Continue to explore Python's extensive libraries and functionalities; the journey from VBA to Python is just the beginning of unlocking the potential that lies within this powerful programming language.

Chapter 12: Best Practices for Python Excel Macros

Leveraging Python for Excel macros not only enhances efficiency but also builds robustness into data manipulation, analysis, and visualization workflows. This chapter delves into best practices for developing, maintaining, and optimizing Python Excel Macros, ensuring that your solutions are not just functional, but also clean, efficient, and scalable.

1. Understanding the Environment

Before diving into best practices, it's essential to grasp the ecosystem. Python integrates with Excel through libraries like `openpyxl`, `pandas`, and `xlwings`. Understanding the strengths and weaknesses of these libraries allows for informed choices during development. For instance:

`pandas` is excellent for data manipulation and analysis but is not geared for direct Excel file manipulation.

`openpyxl` lets you read/write Excel 2010 xlsx/xlsm/xltx/xltm files but lacks advanced features like formula manipulation.

`xlwings` allows for seamless integration with Excel's real-time interaction but requires Excel to be installed on your machine.

Choose libraries based on the specific needs of your project and the environments in which your macros will operate.

2. Maintain Code Scalability and Modularity

As with any programming task, modularity is key. Rather than writing monolithic chunks of code, break your macros down into smaller, reusable functions. This approach facilitates easier debugging, testing, and future enhancements. Here are a few strategies:

Function Design: Design each function to perform a single task. This makes it easier to test individually and reuse in different contexts.

Organize Code in Modules: Group related functions into modules (Python scripts) to keep your project organized. This will make it easier for others (or yourself) to read and maintain the code in the future.

Use Descriptive Naming: Follow consistent and descriptive naming conventions for functions and variables to increase code readability. Opt for names that convey purpose, such as `load_data`, `clean_data`, or `generate_report`.

3. Error Handling

Robust error handling is essential in any application, especially in data processing where unexpected values and conditions may arise. Python's exception handling facilities (`try`, `except`, `finally`) should be utilized to catch and manage errors gracefully. Here are a few considerations:

Validate Inputs: Before processing, validate the data to ensure that it meets expected formats and criteria. This can prevent numerous runtime errors.

Catch Specific Exceptions: Instead of a blanket catch-all, target specific exceptions to handle unique scenarios appropriately. For example, catching a

`FileNotFoundError` when trying to read a file can prompt the user for re-entry.

Logging: Use the `logging` module to record errors and significant events. This not only helps in

diagnosing issues but also serves as a historical log for performance analysis. ## 4. Automate Excel Interactions Judiciously

When automating interactions with Excel, focus on minimizing manual file handling and using efficient read/write operations:

Batch Operations: Instead of writing to Excel cell by cell, collect all the data and write it in bulk. This can notably reduce execution time.

Minimize Screen Updates: If your macro does numerous updates to an Excel file, consider turning off screen updating or calculation until the macro completes its execution. This can improve performance and user experience.

In `xlwings`, for instance, you can do this by:

```python
import xlwings as xw
app = xw.App(visible=False)
workbook = app.books.open('yourfile.xlsx')

# Disable screen updating app.screen_updating = False
```

```
# Code to manipulate Excel


# Re-enable screen updating app.screen_updating = True
` ` `
```

5. Testing and Documentation

The success of any development project hinges on thorough testing and documentation. For Python Excel macros:

Unit Testing: Use libraries like `unittest` or `pytest` to create and run tests for your functions. Write tests for edge cases and common failure scenarios to ensure your macros behave as expected.

Documentation: Document your code with docstrings that explain the purpose of each function, acceptable parameters, return values, and examples of how to use them. Feel free to use tools like Sphinx to generate documentation automatically.

6. Version Control

In collaborative environments or even for personal projects, using version control systems like Git is invaluable. This practice allows you to:

Track changes and understand the evolution of your code.

Collaborate effectively with others by managing branches and merging changes.

Roll back to previous versions in case of bugs or unwanted changes.

Establish a consistent workflow for commits and clearly

comment your changes to foster clarity among collaborators.

7. Optimization and Performance

Finally, optimization is crucial for making your macros not just functional, but also fast. Some optimization techniques include:

Profiling: Use profiling tools like `cProfile` to identify bottlenecks in your code.

Efficient Data Handling: Leverage `pandas` for large datasets, as it is optimized for performance.

Avoid Redundant Calculations: Store intermediate results if they are needed multiple times, rather than recalculating them.

By adhering to the principles outlined in this chapter, you can create robust, efficient, and effective automation solutions that not only save time but also empower users to make informed decisions based on their data. As you progress in your journey of automating Excel tasks with Python, remember that the best code is not just effective, but also comprehensible and maintainable.

Writing Clean and Maintainable Code in Excel with Python

As Excel remains one of the most widely used tools for data analysis, the integration of Python provides additional capabilities that enhance productivity and scalability. Writing clean and maintainable code in this environment is crucial for long-term project success, especially when collaborating with others or returning to your own code after some time. In this chapter, we will explore key principles and practical strategies for writing clean and maintainable Python code in Excel, focusing on readability, organization, documentation, and testing.

1. Understanding the Environment

Before diving into best practices, it's essential to appreciate the environment where Python operates with Excel. Popular libraries like `pandas`, `openpyxl`, and `xlrd` allow users to read, write, and manipulate Excel files. Additionally, tools like `PyXLL` enable seamless integration of Python and Excel, allowing for function calls, event handling, and more. Understanding these environments and leveraging their strengths can lead to cleaner code.

2. Keeping Code Readable

2.1 Clear Naming Conventions

A primary factor in clean code is using clear and descriptive variable and function names. For instance:

Instead of `df`, use `dataframe_sales_data`.

Instead of `calculate()`, use `calculate_total_sales()`.

This practice allows others (and your future self) to understand the purpose of each component quickly. ### 2.2 Consistent Indentation and Formatting

Python relies heavily on indentation, making consistent formatting critical. Use a standard style guide such as PEP 8, which encourages proper spacing, line length, and indentation styles. Utilizing tools like `black` or

`autopep8` can help enforce these standards, ensuring that the codebase remains neat and uniform. ## 3.

194

Structuring Your Code

3.1 Modularization

Breaking down complex functions into smaller, reusable functions is essential. This not only improves readability but also allows for easier testing and debugging. For example, instead of writing a single function that performs multiple tasks, split it into:

`load_data_from_excel(file_path)`

`clean_data(dataframe)`

`calculate_statistics(dataframe)`

This structure not only enhances clarity but also adheres to the DRY (Don't Repeat Yourself) principle. ### 3.2 Directory Structure

When working on larger projects, establishing a clear directory structure can make it easier to navigate the codebase. Consider dividing your project into folders such as `/data`, `/scripts`, `/tests`, and `/docs`. This organization makes it easier for collaborators to find relevant components without sifting through unrelated files.

4. Documenting Your Code ### 4.1 Docstrings

Utilizing docstrings to explain what modules, classes, and functions do is an excellent practice. A function should have a docstring that outlines its parameters, return values, and any exceptions it may raise.

```python
def load_data_from_excel(file_path):
    """
```

195

Load data from an Excel file.

Args:

file_path (str): The path to the Excel file.

Returns:

pandas.DataFrame: The loaded data as a DataFrame.

Raises:

FileNotFoundError: If the file cannot be found. """
```

### 4.2 External Documentation

For more significant projects, consider maintaining an external documentation system, such as Sphinx or MkDocs. This approach allows for comprehensive documentation that includes usage examples, installation guidance, and FAQs.

## 5. Testing and Validation

Testing is a cornerstone of maintainable code, particularly in data-related projects where errors can propagate quickly. Creating unit tests using `unittest` or `pytest` can help ensure that code performs as intended.

### 5.1 Writing Tests

Write tests for each function, ensuring you check for edge cases and potential errors. For instance, if you're testing a function that computes mean values, include tests for empty datasets and datasets with non-numeric entries.

### 5.2 Using Continuous Integration (CI)
```

Employing CI/CD (Continuous Integration/Continuous Deployment) tools, like Travis CI or GitHub Actions, can automate the testing process. Each time code is pushed to the repository, the tests run automatically, helping ensure that new changes do not break existing functionality.

As you integrate Python with Excel, remember that the clarity and maintainability of your code can significantly enhance both your productivity and the quality of the analyses you produce. Embrace these principles, and watch your Python skills flourish in the world of Excel.

Documenting and Version Controlling Your Scripts in Excel with Python

For those who utilize Python alongside Excel, having well-documented code that is systematically version controlled can make a significant difference in productivity and collaboration. This chapter will introduce methods for documenting and version controlling your scripts in Excel using Python. We will cover best practices, tools, and strategies that enhance the readability and maintainability of your scripts while ensuring robust version management.

Why Documenting Scripts is Important ### 1. Clarity and Understanding

Documenting your scripts provides clarity. Well-structured comments and documentation clarify the intent of your code to others and to your future self. Effective documentation explains the purpose of functions, the logic behind complex algorithms, and the significance of variable names.

2. Collaboration

In a collaborative environment, clear documentation is essential. Other team members need to understand your work quickly, allowing them to build upon it or troubleshoot issues effectively. Thorough documentation acts as a roadmap, guiding teammates through your code.

3. Debugging

When issues arise, understanding previous decisions and logic becomes crucial. Comprehensive documentation aids in debugging, enabling you to trace errors and revise your code efficiently.

Best Practices for Documenting Your Scripts ### 1. Use Docstrings

Docstrings are multi-line comments that describe what a function does, its parameters, and its return value. In Python, this is typically done using triple quotes (`"""`).

```python
def calculate_average(data):
"""
```

Calculate the average of a list of numbers.

Parameters:

data (list): A list of numerical values.

Returns:

float: The average of the input numbers. """

```
return sum(data) / len(data)
```

2. In-line Comments

In-line comments help explain specific parts of your code. Use them judiciously to elaborate on complex logic or to highlight the purpose of critical commands.

```python
# Load the Excel file
df = pd.read_excel("data.xlsx")  # Use pandas to read Excel files
```

3. Write Clear and Descriptive Function Names

Descriptive function names improve readability. Aim for names that explain what the function does without requiring extra comments.

```python
def filter_data_by_date(dataframe, start_date, end_date):
# Filter the dataframe between two dates
...
```

4. Keep a Change Log

Maintaining a change log helps track modifications over time. Note significant changes made to your scripts, including bug fixes, new features, and version updates.

```markdown # Change Log
```

Version 1.0.0

Initial script creation for data preprocessing.

Version 1.1.0

Added new function `filter_data_by_date`.

Fixed bug in `calculate_average()`.

```

## Version Control Systems: A Necessity

Using a version control system (VCS) is essential for managing changes to your codebase. The most widely used VCS is Git. Git allows developers to keep track of changes, collaborate with others, and revert to earlier versions when necessary.

### 1. Setting Up Git

**Installation:** Begin by installing Git from [git-scm.com](https://git-scm.com). Follow the installation instructions specific to your operating system.

**Initializing a Repository:** Navigate to your script's directory in the terminal and run:

```bash git init
```

This command creates a new Git repository in that folder.

2. Committing Changes

Once you've set up Git, you can start tracking changes. Use the following command to stage your changes:

```bash

```bash
git add your_script.py
```

Then commit the changes with a meaningful message:

```bash
git commit -m "Added functions for data preprocessing
and Excel interaction."
```

3. Branching

Branches allow you to work on features or fixes without affecting the main codebase. To create a new branch, use:

```bash
git checkout -b new_feature
```

You can switch back to the main branch using:

```bash
git checkout main
```

4. Remote Repositories

To collaborate with others or back up your code, you can use remote repositories. Platforms like GitHub, GitLab, and Bitbucket provide excellent solutions.

To link your local repository to a remote one, use:

```bash
git remote add origin
https://github.com/username/repository.git
```

```
```

After linking, you can push your changes using:

```bash
git push -u origin main
```

Integrating Python with Excel

When working with Excel files, the `pandas` library is an invaluable tool. It allows easy reading and writing of Excel spreadsheets, simplifying data manipulation.

1. Reading From Excel

```python
import pandas as pd

# Load an Excel file into a DataFrame df = pd.read_excel("data.xlsx")

# Display the first few rows print(df.head())
```

2. Writing to Excel

```python
# Save the processed DataFrame to a new Excel file df.to_excel("processed_data.xlsx", index=False)
```

By implementing clear documentation strategies alongside a robust version control system like Git, you ensure that your scripts remain intelligible and easy to navigate. Furthermore, using Python to integrate with Excel can elevate your data analysis and automation capabilities, allowing for more precise and efficient operations. As you progress in your data management journey, continue to refine these skills to maximize your productivity and the quality of your work. Happy coding!

Chapter 13: Troubleshooting and Optimizing Python Excel Scripts

Python has become a popular choice for working with Excel files, thanks to libraries like `pandas`,

`openpyxl`, and `xlrd`. However, as with any programming task, challenges may arise. This chapter aims to equip you with troubleshooting strategies and optimization techniques to enhance your Excel scripts written in Python. By the end, you'll be able to debug more efficiently and improve the performance of your scripts.

13.1 Common Issues and Solutions ### 13.1.1 File Not Found Errors

One of the most frequent issues when working with Excel files is encountering a "File Not Found" error. This can happen for several reasons, including incorrect file paths or misnamed files.

Solution:

Always use absolute paths unless you are certain about the working directory.

Verify that the file name you are trying to access is correct and that the file exists in the specified location.

Example:

```python
import pandas as pd

# Ensure the correct file path file_path = 'C:/path/to/your/file.xlsx' df = pd.read_excel(file_path)
```

```

```

13.1.2 Empty DataFrames

Running a script that reads an Excel file and returns an empty DataFrame can be frustrating. This may occur due to incorrect sheet names, file formats, or empty sheets.

Solution:

Confirm that the specified sheet name exists and is spelled correctly.

Check whether the Excel file has the expected structure and data.

Example:

```python
# Check available sheet names xls = pd.ExcelFile(file_path)

print(xls.sheet_names) # Validate the expected sheet names
```

13.1.3 Data Type Issues

Data type mismatches can lead to errors or incorrect analyses. When reading from Excel, `pandas` attempts to infer data types, but this may not always align with your expectations.

Solution:

Explicitly specify data types when reading in the data.

Clean and validate data after loading.

Example:

```python
df = pd.read_excel(file_path, dtype={'Column1': str, 'Column2': float})
```

Debugging Techniques

13.2.1 Print Statements and Logging

Using print statements is a straightforward way to identify where your script is failing. However, for longer scripts or production code, consider using the `logging` module.

Example:

```python
import logging

logging.basicConfig(level=logging.DEBUG) try:
    df = pd.read_excel(file_path)
    logging.info("Data loaded successfully.") except FileNotFoundError:
    logging.error("The specified file was not found.")
```

13.2.2 Using a Debugger

Python offers several debugging tools, such as `pdb` (Python Debugger). This allows you to step through your code and inspect variables at each step.

Example:

```python import pdb
```

pdb.set_trace()   #   Set   a   breakpoint   df   = pd.read_excel(file_path)

```
```

13.2.3 Unit Tests

Writing unit tests can help you catch bugs early in the development process. Use libraries like `unittest` or

`pytest` to verify the functionality of your scripts.

Example:

```python import unittest
```

class   TestExcelScripts(unittest.TestCase):   def test_data_loading(self):

df = pd.read_excel(file_path)

self.assertFalse(df.empty)   # Ensure DataFrame is not empty

if __name__ == '__main__':

unittest.main()

```
```

13.3 Performance Optimization

Performance becomes critical as your scripts process larger datasets. Here are several techniques to improve efficiency:

207

13.3.1 Use the Appropriate Library

Choose the right library based on your needs. For heavy data manipulation, `pandas` is often preferred due to its efficiency and ease of use.

13.3.2 Read and Write Efficiently

Use memory-efficient options when reading/writing Excel files. For example, when dealing with large files, consider using `chunk_size` in `pandas`.

Example:

```python
for chunk in pd.read_excel(file_path, chunksize=10000):

process_chunk(chunk)
```

13.3.3 Optimize DataFrames

Before performing operations on DataFrames, make sure that unnecessary columns or rows are dropped. This not only reduces memory usage but can also speed up

operations.

Example:

```python
df.drop(columns=['unnecessary_column'], inplace=True)
```

13.3.4 Use Vectorized Operations

Leverage `pandas` vectorization for operations whenever possible instead of iterating through rows.

Example:

```python
df['new_column'] = df['existing_column'] * 10  # Vectorized operation
```

Understanding how to troubleshoot and optimize your Python Excel scripts is crucial for efficient data manipulation and analysis. By familiarizing yourself with common issues, debugging techniques, and optimization strategies, you can develop scripts that run smoothly and effectively handle your data tasks.

Remember, coding is an iterative process; continually test and refine your scripts, and don't hesitate to consult community resources or documentation whenever you encounter challenges. With practice, your skills will grow and enhance your overall experience with Python and Excel.

Identifying and Resolving Bottlenecks in Excel with python

These bottlenecks may manifest as slow loading times, lagging calculations, or even application freezes, especially when handling large datasets or complex formulas. In this chapter, we will explore how to identify and resolve these performance-related issues using Python, specifically focusing on leveraging libraries such as `pandas`, `openpyxl`, and `xlrd` to analyze and optimize Excel files.

Section 1: Understanding Bottlenecks in Excel

Before diving into solutions, it is crucial to understand what constitutes a bottleneck in Excel. Bottlenecks can arise from various factors:

Large Data Volumes: Excel struggles with large datasets, particularly those exceeding 1 million rows.

Complex Formulas: Nested formulas or excessive use of volatile functions (like `NOW()`,

`RAND()`, or `OFFSET()`) can contribute significantly to slow performance.

Inefficient Data Structures: The way data is organized (e.g., unstructured tables) can affect Excel's ability to process information quickly.

Conditional Formatting and Graphics: Overuse of conditional formatting and embedded graphics can also be a source of slow performance.

Section 2: Identifying Bottlenecks with Python ### 2.1 Analyzing Excel Files

To identify bottlenecks, we can use Python's `pandas` library to read and analyze Excel files efficiently. First, we need to install the necessary libraries:

```bash
pip install pandas openpyxl xlrd
```

Here's a sample code snippet that loads an Excel file and summarizes its contents:

```python
import pandas as pd
# Load an Excel file
file_path = 'path_to_your_excel_file.xlsx' xls = pd.ExcelFile(file_path)
# Get the names of all sheets sheet_names = xls.sheet_names print(f"Sheet Names: {sheet_names}")
# Summarize the contents of each sheet for sheet in sheet_names:
df = pd.read_excel(xls, sheet_name=sheet) print(f"Summary of {sheet}:") print(df.info())
```

This script will provide a high-level overview of each sheet, including the number of rows, data types, and missing values. By analyzing the output, we can pinpoint which sheets are the largest and may likely cause performance issues.

2.2 Identifying Slow Formulas

Although Python won't evaluate Excel formulas directly, we can extract formulas from the Excel sheet and check for potential inefficiencies. By looking for nested or volatile formulas, we can create a filter to identify which cells might be contributing to slow performance.

```python
# Extract formulas from the sheet and identify potential bottlenecks def extract_formulas(sheet_name):

df = pd.read_excel(xls, sheet_name=sheet_name, engine='openpyxl')

formulas = df.applymap(lambda x: x if isinstance(x, str) and x.startswith('=') else None) return formulas

# Iterate through all sheets and print formula details for sheet in sheet_names:

formulas_df = extract_formulas(sheet) print(f"Formulas in {sheet}:") print(formulas_df.dropna())
```

This code retrieves all formulas from each sheet and allows us to assess whether any repetitive or complex formulas exist.

Section 3: Resolving Bottlenecks ### 3.1 Optimizing Data Structure

One of the most effective ways to resolve bottlenecks is by ensuring data is well-structured. Excel functions best with a clear tabular format. Consider using `pandas` to clean and structure your data effectively.

For instance, we can normalize data by removing any unnecessary or duplicate columns:

```python
# Normalize Data: Drop unnecessary columns for sheet in sheet_names:

df = pd.read_excel(xls, sheet_name=sheet) # Drop duplicate or unnecessary columns df = df.loc[:, ~df.columns.duplicated()]

# Export cleaned data back to Excel df.to_excel(f'cleaned_{sheet}.xlsx', index=False)
```

3.2 Reducing Formula Complexity

To tackle complex formulas, consider breaking them into simpler components or using helper columns. Additionally, leveraging Python for pre-calculating values before writing them back to Excel can significantly reduce calculation time.

```python
# Pre-calculate values using Python and write back to Excel
```

```
for sheet in sheet_names:

df = pd.read_excel(xls, sheet_name=sheet)

# Assuming we are simplifying a complex column if
'complex_formula_column' in df.columns:

df['optimized_column']                      =
df['complex_formula_column'].apply(lambda        x:
pre_calculation(x))
df.drop(columns=['complex_formula_column'],
inplace=True)          df.to_excel(f'optimized_{sheet}.xlsx',
index=False)

```
```

3.3 Dynamic Data Validation

Ensure that validation rules are streamlined. Overuse of data validation can bog down performance, so it's best to minimize checks wherever possible. This can be accomplished directly in Excel or by preprocessing data in Python.

The methods outlined in this chapter not only enhance Excel's performance but also empower users to leverage Python's capabilities for smarter data management, ultimately driving productivity and efficiency. As businesses increasingly rely on data-driven decision-making, mastering these techniques becomes indispensable for any data analyst or manager.
```

Conclusion

In this comprehensive exploration of Python Excel Macros Script, we have journeyed through the intricacies of harnessing the power of Python to automate tasks within Excel. Our discussions have ranged from the foundational concepts of Excel and Python scripting to more advanced applications, demonstrating how you can streamline your workflows and enhance productivity.

By learning to create and deploy Python scripts that manipulate Excel spreadsheets, you've equipped yourself with a powerful tool to tackle repetitive tasks with ease. Whether you're a data analyst, a business professional, or a hobbyist, the skills and techniques outlined in this eBook will enable you to maximize the potential of Excel far beyond its conventional limits.

As we conclude, it's important to remember that the landscape of programming and automation is ever-evolving. Embracing continuous learning and experimentation will empower you to discover new ways to leverage Python and Excel together. We encourage you to explore additional libraries such as `Pandas`,

`OpenPyXL`, and `xlwings`, and stay updated with the latest trends and updates in the Python ecosystem.

Your journey doesn't end here; we invite you to take what you've learned and start creating your own projects. The practical application of these concepts will reinforce your skills and inspire you to push the boundaries of what is possible with Python and Excel.

Thank you for joining us on this journey. We hope that the insights and techniques shared in this eBook will serve you well in your pursuits, transforming the way you interact with data through automation.

Biography

Bryan Singer is a seasoned expert in the world of Singer, bringing years of dedicated study and hands-on experience to the table. As the author of this comprehensive eBook, Bryan combines his deep understanding of the subject with a passion for sharing knowledge, making even the most complex topics accessible and engaging for readers.

With a background in web development and a knack for creating innovative web applications, Bryan's technical prowess is undeniable. He has a strong command of Python, leveraging its power to develop cutting-edge solutions that solve real-world problems. Additionally, Bryan's proficiency in Excel and data management tools adds another layer of expertise, ensuring that his insights are not only theoretically sound but also practically applicable.

When he's not immersed in the digital world, Bryan enjoys exploring the ever-evolving landscape of technology. His hobbies include tinkering with new programming languages, staying updated with the latest trends in web development, and experimenting with innovative ways to enhance user experiences online.

Bryan's commitment to continuous learning and improvement is reflected in his writing, where he blends technical rigor with a relatable, down-to-earth style. His goal is to empower readers to harness the full potential of Singer, enabling them to achieve their objectives with confidence and efficiency.

Dive into Bryan Singer's eBook and discover a treasure trove of knowledge that will transform your understanding and application of Singer. With his expertise guiding you, the possibilities are endless.

Glossary: Python Excel Macros Scripts

A

API (Application Programming Interface)

A set of protocols and tools that allow different software applications to communicate with each other. In the context of Python and Excel, APIs enable Python scripts to interact with Excel files and perform various operations.

B

Backend

The server-side of an application, managing data processing and storage. In Excel macros, the backend may refer to the hidden processes that execute when a user runs a macro.

C

Cell

The intersection of a row and a column in an Excel worksheet. Cells are the basic units of storage in Excel where data, formulas, or values reside.

CSV (Comma-Separated Values)

A file format used to store tabular data, where each line corresponds to a row and each value is separated by a comma. Python can read and write CSV files using libraries such as `pandas`.

D

DataFrame

A data structure used in the popular Python library `pandas`, designed to handle and manipulate data in a table-like format. DataFrames are essential for data analysis tasks involving Excel data.

Dependency

In programming, a dependency refers to a library or module that is required for another script or module to function correctly. Python scripts may depend on libraries like `openpyxl`, `pandas`, or `xlwings` to interact with Excel.

E

ExcelFile

An object provided by the `pandas` library that is used to read from and write to Excel files. It allows loading multiple sheets and performing data manipulation efficiently.

Macro

A sequence of instructions that automate repetitive tasks in Excel. While macros are typically written in VBA, Python scripts can serve as macros to automate workflows in a more flexible manner.

xlwings

A Python library that makes it easy to call Python from Excel and vice versa. It integrates Excel with Python, allowing for dynamic interaction and automation of Excel tasks.

F

Function

In Python, a function is a block of reusable code that performs a specific task. Functions can be defined to carry out operations on Excel data, such as calculations or formatting.

G

Gelato

A term not typically used in programming but could be referenced as a metaphor for the sweetness and satisfaction derived from successfully automating processes and deriving insights from data.

H

Hyperlink

A clickable link embedded in a cell that redirects to another location, either within the same workbook or to an external resource. Python can manipulate hyperlinks in Excel using relevant libraries.

I

Import

The process of bringing external libraries or modules into a Python script. This allows access to their functionalities, such as reading Excel files or manipulating data.

Iteration

The process of cycling through a collection of items (like rows in a sheet) to process or analyze them one at a time. Python's for-loops make it easy to iterate over data structures, including Excel worksheets.

J

JSON (JavaScript Object Notation)

A lightweight format for data interchange that is easy for humans to read and write. Python scripts can convert Excel data to JSON for web integration or API communication.

L

Library

A collection of pre-written code that provides reusable functionalities. Python has a robust ecosystem of libraries (such as `pandas`, `numpy`, and `openpyxl`) that facilitate Excel automation and data analysis.

M

Module

A file containing Python code that can define functions, classes, and variables. Python modules can be imported into scripts to enhance functionality and maintain organization.

pandas

A powerful Python library that provides data structures and data analysis tools. It is particularly known for its DataFrame object and is widely used for data

manipulation, including working with Excel files.

O

OpenPyXL

A Python library for reading and writing Excel 2010 xlsx/xlsm/xltx/xltm files. It enables Python scripts to create new Excel files, modify existing ones, and perform complex data manipulations.

P

Pandas Excel Writer

A function in the `pandas` library that allows writing DataFrames to Excel files. It can create new sheets and add data to existing sheets effectively.

PyAutoGUI

A Python library that provides control over the mouse and keyboard. It can be utilized to automate GUI interactions with Excel applications where scripting isn't sufficient.

R

Row

A horizontal line of cells in an Excel worksheet, identified by a number. Rows contain data points relevant to the proceeding categories identified by columns.

S

Script

A series of commands written in Python that performs tasks automatically. Scripts can contain functions, loops, and conditional statements to handle Excel data manipulation.

`openpyxl`

A Python library designed to read/write Excel 2010 xlsx/xlsm/xltx/xltm files. It allows for extensive interaction with Excel, including cell manipulation, formatting, and chart creation.

T

Tuple

An immutable sequence of Python objects, often used to store related data. In the context of Excel, tuples may represent rows, where each element corresponds to a cell in that row.

U

User Defined Functions (UDF)

Functions that are created by a user in Excel. When leveraging Python, users can create UDFs to perform complex calculations not available through standard Excel functions.

V

Variable

A symbolic name associated with a value that can change during the execution of a script. Variables are essential in Python scripts for storing data extracted from Excel.

W

Workbook

A collection of one or more worksheets in Excel. When using Python, a workbook is often an object representing the Excel file being manipulated.

Worksheet

A single spreadsheet within a workbook that contains rows and columns of data. Python interacts with worksheets to extract, modify, or analyze data.